19.86

Many HAPPY RETURNS

D

BUDGERIGARS
IN COLOUR

Their Care and Breeding

By A. RUTGERS

English Edition
edited by Cyril H. Rogers, F.B.S.A.

With 64 illustrations by
K. J. Heinzel and R. A. Vowles

BLANDFORD PRESS
POOLE DORSET

First published in the U.K. in 1958 as *The Care and Breeding of Budgerigars*
by Blandford Press
Link House, West Street
Poole, Dorset BH15 1LL

Completely revised, 1967
2nd edition (revised) 1970
3rd edition (revised) 1973
4th edition (revised) 1976
Reprinted 1979
Reprinted 1982
Reprinted 1983
5th edition (revised) 1986

ISBN 0 7137 0813 1

Based on
Handboek voor Kleurparkietenwekers

Distributed in the United States by
Sterling Publishing Co., Inc.,
2 Park Avenue, New York, N.Y. 10016

ACKNOWLEDGMENTS

The publishers wish to acknowledge the permission given by The Budgerigar Society, 49–53, Hazelwood Road, Northampton, to include the illustrations of the B.S. Standard Show Cage (p. 145), the British Standard Ideal Cock (p. 13), and also their Scale of Points and Standard for the Ideal Budgerigar (p. 140 and p. 142) and Colour Standard (p. 14).

Printed in Hong Kong by South China Printing Co.

CONTENTS

PREFACE *page* 4

PART ONE—CARE

1 THE BUDGERIGAR IN AUSTRALIA 5
2 DEVELOPMENT 8
3 THE COLOUR STANDARDS OF THE BUDGERIGAR SOCIETY 12

THE COLOUR PLATES 32
4 ACCOMMODATION IN CAGES AND AVIARIES 97
5 FEEDING 114
6 DISEASES 118
7 REPRODUCTION 124
8 APPLIANCES FOR CAGES AND AVIARIES 134
9 BUDGERIGARS ON SHOW 139
10 TRAINING BUDGERIGARS AND TEACHING THEM TO TALK 148

PART TWO—BREEDING

11 COLOUR CHARACTERS 156
12 THE NORMAL VARIETIES 163
13 YELLOW-WINGS AND WHITEWINGS (THE CLEAR-WING GROUP) 167
14 THE YELLOW-FACED BLUE SERIES 171
15 THE FALLOWS 174
16 THE VIOLET CHARACTER 177
17 RECESSIVE DANISH PIEDS 181
18 CONTINENTAL CLEAR-FLIGHTED AND DUTCH PIEDS 184
19 THE DARK-EYED CLEAR WHITES AND DARK-EYED CLEAR YELLOWS 187
20 DOMINANT AUSTRALIAN PIEDS 190
21 THE CRESTED TYPES 194
22 NEWLY ESTABLISHED VARIETIES 198
23 SOME OTHER VARIETIES 199
APPENDIX: COLOUR PERCENTAGE TABLES 205
BIBLIOGRAPHY 238
INDEX 241

PREFACE

Budgerigars were first introduced into Great Britain in 1840, some 145 years ago, and during this period they have become tremendous favourites as household pets, aviary and exhibition birds, not only in Europe but also all over the world.

During their time of breeding in captivity the Native Light Green Budgerigars have given rise to quite a multitude of mutant colours which very much increased their popularity amongst aviculturists. These colour varieties range from pure white to deep blue and violet and pure golden yellow to dark green and olive green. In addition to all the mutant colours, there are different feather patterns with varying depth of shade and black, plum and red coloured eyes, and of course an incredible number of composite coloured birds.

Because there are so many different colour forms breeders cannot keep all of them so they specialise in various groups of colours, and this has been the means of substantially improving these colours. To be able to breed colours it is essential for Fanciers to have some knowledge of the mechanism of inheritance as well as an expertise in keeping, breeding and exhibiting these charming little Australian Parrakeets.

In many Chapters of this book readers will find particulars of how to recognise the different colour forms when read in conjunction with the large number of Colour Plates. Their breeding habits are given in some detail in simple straightforward language so they can be easily understood.

The purpose of this book is to give Fanciers easy access to all aspects of keeping Budgerigars and will enable them to build up healthy vigorous strains of their selected colours and to preserve and establish any new mutations.

PART ONE

CARE

1. THE BUDGERIGAR IN AUSTRALIA

On one of his journeys of discovery into the vast expanse of inner Australia, John Gould chanced upon one of the smallest breeds of parrots, the *Melopsittacus Undulatus* as Shaw named it afterwards. Shaw was the first scientist to know and describe the Budgerigar.

The explanation of the name is easy, *Melos* being the Greek for song and *Psittakos* for parrot. *Undulatus* is the Latin for wave-lined. The French and German names, *perruche ondule* and *Wellensittich* respectively, also refer to the wavy pattern of the bird's plumage, but the English word Budgerigar is a corruption of the Australian Aboriginal name 'Betcherrygah' which, roughly speaking, means 'good food'. It is a remarkable fact that these birds lead a truly nomadic life, appearing suddenly in parts where the magic of heavy rains has turned the desert into one vast, luxurious meadow. Like other birds, the Budgerigar seems to possess a special instinct, informing it of such an occurrence long enough beforehand, for it always appears at the feeding grounds at the right moment. In former years the name of 'Undulated Grass Parakeet' seems to have been in frequent use, and the Dutch designation *Grasparkiet* is certainly derived from that description.

As early as 1831, the museum of the London Linnean Society showed a then unique specimen, a stuffed Grass Parakeet; at that time no one could have predicted that, a century later, millions of these birds, in a vast variety of colours, would be kept as domestic pets all over Europe and in every other part of the world.

Neither could Gould possibly have foreseen such developments when, in 1840, he brought Budgerigars to England.

If Shaw had been the first to describe the birds, the credit of having given the first accurate account of their habits and ways of life belongs to Gould who described them in his famous work *The Birds of Australia* (1840–1848).

Gould watched large numbers of the birds in the vast plains of Inner Australia where, during the hottest hours of the afternoon, they kept silently hidden in the foliage of the gum trees. In the morning and evening, however, they flew merrily among the tops of the trees and repaired, in flocks of 20 to 100, to their watering places. In the morning, they also went to their feeding grounds. That was in the month of December, and they were busily hatching out their eggs in the Eucalyptus trees and producing entire colonies of nestlings. Brehm received more detailed reports from Engelhardt, from which I quote the following:

'Among the more incidental guests of Southern Australia is the beloved Grass Parakeet. One of its favourite haunts where, incidentally, I made my immediate observations, is the Eucalyptus wood, the *Mallee shrub* situated on the brinks of the Murray between its mouth and the first big curve. When, in this inhospitable region, a wet winter is followed by heavy rains continuing well into spring, i.e. into the end of September and on into October, the grass will shoot upwards attaining a density and height otherwise unknown. Countless square miles of usually desolate desert sand are then covered with exquisite kangaroo grass which, under the influence of the warm rays of the sun, will grow to a height of fully three to five feet. Its subtropical bloom will develop quickly, and after a mere five to six weeks the ears will be carrying seeds. Long before this, though, countless swarms of Grass Parakeets will have made their appearance beginning busily to make nests right away. The singular way of growth peculiar to the Mallee distinctly favours such ambitions. Eight to twelve trunks, everyone of them some 18 feet in height, will usually sprout from a single root stock. Each of those trunks is covered with white bark and adorned with very scanty foliage. To make up for that, it will show countless knot-holes. Every hollow trunk, every shoulder and, in case of need, every appropriate hollow between the roots will now be used for nesting purposes. Inside a few weeks, the country will regularly be teeming with Parakeets, and nobody will deny that the ripening grass seeds are perfectly suited to feeding the young. Anyone happening to pass such a spot at this time would be able to catch the young easily with his bare hands! They will fly up from the grass at his feet and, amidst loud chatter, will perch in long rows on the bare branches of the trees.

'As soon as the opulence of the seeds begins to wane or if a lack of water threatens, their roving instinct will prevail again, and they will vanish as suddenly as they came making for the Alexandra and Wellington lakes the Murray crosses before reaching the sea. It was mainly in those regions they used to be caught by the thousand in the nets of the bird catchers.

'This picture however, only applies to the years of abundant rains. In other years when the rainfall remains considerably below the average, they seem to have vanished altogether. It is almost certain they have then flown further North, where often, in the summer heat, violent thunder showers occur which, as though by magic, will turn sandy deserts into grassy plains. The roving parrots seem to foreknow this and invariably put in an appearance where the table is well-furnished.'

Cayley has little to add. He informs us that the spring or the end of the winter is the usual time for the Budgerigars to arrive in the southern parts of Australia, and that, already in March, or even as early as February, they will fly north again. Further he stresses their charming, merry chatter and their lively, graceful ways. Their flight is straight and fast and accompanied by shrill sounds. He indicates their breeding time as usually from October till December, and they lay from four to eight eggs, pure white in colour.

Other naturalists state that Budgerigars never move further south than Melbourne and are seldom seen on the coast. They are also absent from Tasmania.

Although the birds may make do with hollow dead timber they prefer making their nests in live Eucalyptus and gum trees. The hollows are apt to vary considerably in depth, reaching a depth of from 6 in. to 16 in. (13–40 cm) with an entrance of from 1½ in. to 2 in. (4–5 cm) wide. No nesting material whatever is used.

When migrating to other parts flocks will often merge into one huge concourse sometimes covering so large an area that the light of the sun is obscured by flying Budgerigars. It seems to be established that they do not return to the same habitats in the same season year by year. A region accommodating thousands one season may see very few of them in the next. Budgerigars appear to suffer severely in abnormally hot weather; heat waves in Australia account for numerous victims.

In view of the large number of colour varieties we have come to know, it is not at all surprising to learn that mutants have been observed in the wild. Apart from the Light Greens, we know a variety which Cayley called the *Melopsittacus undulatus intermedius* and described as follows:

'Differs from the *Melopsittacus undulatus* by a more pallid colour, especially in the neck and on the back, whereas on the top and on the underside they are darker than the *Melopsittacus undulatus pallidiceps* succeeding it. It seems to occur mainly in the Northern Territory.'

The *Melopsittacus undulatus pallidiceps* occurring in Western Australia differs from the *Melopsittacus undulatus* mainly by the lighter colour of its head. But there is no doubt there are wild specimens of the Dark Greens and of the Light Yellows. The former may be found in the Natural History Museum in Kensington; the latter were repeatedly reported by eye-witnesses as flying in a flock swarming to the watering place.

To anyone knowing the care necessary to preserve a mutant it must be obvious that mutants are bound to disappear rather quickly when living in the wild. In the second part of this work, we shall revert to this question in considerable detail.

2. DEVELOPMENT

We may follow the Budgerigar's process of domestication more closely than that of any other pet. Many a theory has been ventured concerning the origin of cats and dogs, horses, sheep and cows, but we do not possess complete genealogical tables covering the descent of any of these animals and are thus unable to trace the source of the mutants in type and colour. Our knowledge of the laws governing the apparent caprices of heredity has resulted from endless labour on the part of biologists; even now the science of heredity is still young and its unsolved problems are many.

So far as the Budgerigar is concerned, we know practically all the essential facts since the day when it was brought to Europe, including those covering the first colour mutants.

John Gould, a famous ornithologist, brought the first Budgerigars to England in 1840. For years he and his wife traversed Australia from the north to the south and from the east to the west to gather material for his book on *The Birds of Australia*, a magnificent work wonderfully illustrated with pictures painted by his wife. Before this, a stuffed specimen had been brought home from a journey to the fifth continent and, since then has belonged to the collection of the museum of the Linnean Society of London; but before this, no living Budgerigars had been imported. The birds Gould brought with him had been bred in a cage by his brother-in-law.

The bird dealer Jamrach of London sold the first pair for £27! As early as 1850 Budgerigars are known to have been exhibited at the Antwerp Zoo. At that time the Antwerp Zoo was the centre of the European bird trade and it used to organize big yearly bird auctions, booking orders from as far away as Berlin and St. Petersburg. Belgium and Holland, so near to this centre, naturally turned into the pioneers of Budgerigar breeding.

The understandable favour the small, graceful, lively and charming little parakeets met with on the part of all bird fanciers, soon made the Budgerigar trade soar to such heights that it was difficult for bird catchers in Australia to keep pace with the enormous demand. The fact that France alone required 100,000 pairs a year, will furnish an idea of the numbers shipped. As soon as it was clear that once the birds had become acclimatized they were easy to keep and breed, a number of enterprising Frenchmen took up breeding on a wholesale basis. In and around Toulouse, where the climate was exceptionally suitable for these purposes, a number of breeding establishments acquired considerable importance. Among these may be mentioned the *Etablissements Bastide* founded in 1880 and the *Etablissements Ornithologiques Blanchard* in 1886. Both of them kept 80,000 to 100,000 birds!

As Nature endowed its creatures with a tendency to create variations, it was only natural that mutants should occur. Man is too easily inclined to ascribe such mutants not only to a change of living conditions but also to selection and in breeding. Nor can it be denied that, knowing what we do nowadays, we are able to take a hand in such development. But we should never overlook the fact that the tendency to breed variations is an attribute of Nature itself and that, without this potential variability, the results we see today could never have been attained. Bearing this in mind it was to be expected that the first mutants occurring in the breeders' aviaries would also have had precedents in nature, and subsequent investigations and eye-witness reports established that, now and then, a flock of wild Light Greens will embrace an occasional Yellow. In its natural state a mutant will scarcely be able to hold its ground; the Yellows are bound to be soon absorbed by the Greens. Our knowledge of the laws of heredity, however, enabled us to preserve the mutant in its domesticated state and to forge it into the first link of the endless chain of colours and colour varieties which characterize the Budgerigar family today. In its natural environment, when the Yellow is mated with one of the Greens, all the chicks turn out to be Greens. But man mated the Yellow back to its offspring and thus preserved the new colour factor.

With the appearance of the first yellow coloured mutants (1872 in Belgium, and 1875 in Germany), the interest of scientists was aroused and for the first time science was in a position to follow closely a hereditary process. As early as 1879, in Uccle in Belgium, the Lutino appeared, but being represented exclusively by hens, it disappeared almost as quickly as it had come. In England, the Lutino did not occur until 1884, when Abrahams was the fortunate possessor, but this strain was not established.

Booms occur frequently where breeding produces rarities. Holland knew its bulb boom, and the Budgerigar trade witnessed a modest Yellow boom. Yellows were soon sold at considerable prices. Enterprising gentlemen managed to produce a definite 'corner' in Yellows and made profits accordingly.

As early as 1886 Abrahams stated that his bird catchers in Australia had sighted some Yellows among the Greens. He even received some of them from Australia. The reports of those days mainly mentioned Yellow hens; Abrahams reported the reception of a Yellow cock. As it is certain that there must have been normal Yellow cocks, we are now inclined to suppose these reports actually concerned Lutinos. Perhaps the fanciers failed to pay sufficient attention to the eyes. It seems strange that the first breeders should have got nothing but Yellow hens! Where Lutinos are concerned such results would be quite in order.

Again in Belgium, and again in Uccle, the first Blue was produced. It took some time, however, for the Blues to hold their ground, and it was not until 1910 that the first pair could be exhibited at a show at the Royal Horticultural Hall, in Westminster. After the First World War, the French produced Blues again and contributed a lot to their development. In 1921, the first Blue was reported in Germany.

Like the Yellows, the Blues are Green 'Sports' and should occur in the wild, but up till now no wild Blue has ever been reported. However, a wild Blue mutant of the Green Quaker Parakeet can be seen at several European Zoos.

Meanwhile theoreticians who had studied the science of heredity in general, and that of colour heredity in particular, had contended that a White variety was bound to crop up sooner or later, and sure enough reports of Whites soon began to pour in from the aviaries breeding Blues, Yellows and Greens together. The first Whites occurred simultaneously both in England and France during 1920 and in both cases were bred from Blues that had yellow ancestry.

It is of some importance to point out this was the first case of a variety hardly likely to occur in the wild where Yellow and Blue mutants are rarer and, anyway, never hold their ground. Under the guidance of man those colours, now preserved, offered an array of fascinating possibilities which breeders began to explore.

Even before the Yellows and the Blues put in an appearance, it had been established that the Greens showed distinct differences, through the existence of a Dark factor turning the Light Greens to dark or olive green. France presented us with the three different shades of Greens. These three shades, afterwards designated as Light, Medium and Dark, representing birds without a dark factor, with one dark factor and with two dark factors, respectively, were found to be repeated in the other colour varieties. That is why nowadays, we have got Sky Blues, Cobalts and Mauves. The same shades prevail among the Yellows and the Whites, although, of course, in these varieties it is not so easy to distinguish them.

The boom periods are past, and although fashion and taste will occasionally produce a sudden popularity for a new colour variety so that its price will soar, such disproportionate rises are always short-lived. The gains and losses such ventures involve are the concern of professional breeders alone.

Those serving and honouring the hobby for its own sake will specialize on a certain colour and a certain colour combination that, for some reason or other, happens to win their affection, and their sole aim will be to breed birds that, in type as well as in colour, will be as near perfect as possible. Naturally there is always the possibility that one may succeed in creating a new colour and this possibility will never cease to be a special attraction. But nothing should be left to chance. The breeder will have to take the trouble of making a close study of the laws of heredity as well as of the structure of the plumage and, last but not least, he will have to acquire an intimate knowledge of the colour factors.

Most of the Budgerigars we see nowadays differ in size, from the wild Australian type. One of the foremost of British bird lovers, the late Duke of Bedford, pointed this out in connection with his experiments. These led him to allow his Budgerigars to fly about freely in his park. In doing so, he discovered that the length of the wings of free flying, and consequently free breeding, birds was smaller than the usual length shown by birds bred in cages. The body of the wild bird, too, is shorter than that of the aviary specimen. But we may also happen upon divergences in the opposite direction, where the birds bred from young parents were too small.

3. THE COLOUR STANDARDS OF THE BUDGERIGAR SOCIETY

Light Green Pl. 1

Mask, buttercup of an even tone ornamented by six evenly spaced large round black throat spots, the outer two being partially covered at the base by cheek patches. *Cheek patches*, violet. *General body colour*, back, rump, breast, flanks and underparts, bright grass-green of a solid and even shade throughout. *Markings*, on cheeks, back of head, neck and wings, black and well defined on a buttercup ground. *Tail*, long feathers, blue-black. *Eye*, black with white iris. *Feet and legs*, blue/grey mottled.

British Standard Ideal

Dark Green Pl. 2

As above but with a dark laurel green body colour. *Tail,* long feathers darker in proportion.

Olive Green Pl. 3

As above but with a deep olive green body colour. *Tail,* long feathers darker in proportion.

Grey Green Pl. 4

This variety conforms to the standard for Light Green except in the following details: *Cheek patches,* grey. *General body colour,* dull mustard green. *Tail,* long feathers, black.

NOTE. There are Light, Medium and Dark forms of the Grey Green.

Light Yellow Pl. 5

Mask, buttercup yellow. *Cheek patches,* silvery white. *General body colour,* back, rump, breast, flanks and underparts, deep buttercup yellow and as free from green suffusion as possible. *Primaries and tail,* lighter than body. *Eye,* black with a white iris. *Feet and legs,* blue/grey mottled.

Dark Yellow

As above but correspondingly deeper in colour.

Olive Yellow

As above but correspondingly deeper in colour.

Grey Yellow

The Grey Yellow conforms to the standard for Light Yellow except in the following details: *Cheek patches,* pale grey. *General body colour,* dull mustard yellow. *Primaries and tail,* off white to pale grey. (It should be noted that there are light, medium, and dark forms of the Grey Yellow.)

Yellow (suffused)

Mask, yellow, ornamented by six evenly spaced large round very pale grey throat spots, the outer two being partially covered by the base of the cheek patches. *Cheek patches,* very pale blue to pale violet. *General body colour,* back, rump, breast and flanks and underparts yellow, suffused, with a dilute shade of the colour being masked. *Wings and tail,* white, bluish or light grey. *Eye*, black with a white iris. *Feet and legs*, blue/grey mottled. (It should be noted that there are light, dark and olive green shades in both light and dark suffusion.)

Sky Blue Pl. 7

Mask, clear white ornamented by six evenly spaced large round black throat spots, the outer two being partially covered at the base by cheek patches. *Cheek patches*, violet. *General body colour*, back, rump, breast, flanks and underparts, pure skyblue. *Markings*, on cheeks, back of head, neck and wings, black and well defined on a white ground. *Tail*, long feathers, deep blue. *Feet and legs*, blue/grey mottled. *Eye*, black with a white isis.

Cobalt Pl. 8

As above but with a rich deep cobalt blue body colour. *Tail*, long feathers darker in proportion.

Mauve Pl. 9

As above but with a purplish mauve, body colour with a tendency to a pinkish tone. *Tail*, long feathers darker in proportion.

Violet Cobalt Pl. 10

As above but with a deep intense violet body colour. *Tail*, long feathers darker in proportion.

Grey

The Grey conforms to the standard for Skyblue except in the following details: *Cheek patches*, grey. *General body colour*, grey. *Tail*, long feathers black. (It should be noted that there are light, medium and dark shades of grey.)

White (suffused)

Mask, white, ornamented by six evenly spaced large round very pale grey throat spots, the outer two being partially covered by the base of the cheek patches. *Cheek patches*, very pale blue to pale violet (pale grey in the grey variety). *General body colour*, back, rump, breast, flanks and underparts white suffused with a dilute shade of the colour being masked. *Wings and tail*, white bluish or light grey. *Eye*, black with a white iris. *Feet and legs*, blue/grey mottled. (It should be noted that there are skyblue, cobalt, mauve, violet and grey shades in both light and dark suffusion.)

Yellow-wing Light Green

Mask, buttercup yellow. *Cheek patches*, violet. *General body colour*, back, rump, breast, flanks and underparts bright grass green of an even colour throughout, approximating to the normal variety in depth and intensity. *Primary flight feathers*, off white. *Wings*, buttercup yellow as free from markings as possible. *Tail*, long feathers blue. *Feet and legs*, blue/grey mottled. *Eye*, black with a white iris.

Yellow-wing Dark Green

As above but with a laurel green body colour. *Tail*, long feathers darker in proportion.

Yellow-wing Olive Green

As above but with an olive green body colour. *Tail*, long feathers darker in proportion.

Yellow-wing Grey Green

The Yellow-wing Grey Green conforms to the standard for Yellow-wing Light Green except in the following details: *Cheek patches*, grey. *General body colour*, dull mustard green. *Tail*, grey. (It should be noted that there are light, medium and dark forms of Yellow-wing Grey Green.)

Greywing Light Green

Mask, buttercup yellow, ornamented by six evenly spaced large round grey throat spots, the outer two being partially covered by the base of the cheek patches. *Cheek patches*, light violet. *General body colour*, back, rump, breast, flanks and underparts bright grass green, 50% of normal body colour depth. *Markings*, on cheeks, back of head, neck and wings should be light grey well defined on a yellow ground. *Tail*, long feathers grey with bluish tinge. *Feet and legs*, blue/grey mottled. *Eye*, black with a white iris.

Greywing Dark Green

As above but with a light laurel green body colour. *Tail*, long feathers darker in proportion.

Greywing Olive Green

As above but with a light olive green body colour. *Tail*, long feathers darker still in proportion.

Greywing Grey Green

As above but with a light mustard green body colour. *Check patches*, light grey. *Tail*, long feathers dark grey.

Greywing Skyblue

Mask, white, ornamented by six evenly spaced large round grey throat spots, the outer two being partially covered by the base of the cheek patches. *Cheek patches*, light violet. *General body colour*, back, rump, breast, flanks and underparts pure skyblue. 50% of normal body colour depth. *Markings*, on cheeks, back of head, neck and wings should be light grey well defined on a white ground. *Tail*, long feathers grey with bluish tinge. *Feet and legs*, blue/grey mottled. *Eye*, black with a white iris.

Greywing Cobalt

As above but with a pale cobalt body colour. *Tail*, long feathers darker in proportion.

Greywing Violet Cobalt

As above but with a pale violet body colour. *Tail*, long feathers darker in proportion.

Greywing Mauve

As above but with a pale mauve body colour. *Tail*, long feathers darker in proportion.

Greywing Grey

As above but with a pale grey body colour. *Check patches*, pale grey. *Tail*, long feathers dark grey.

Cinnamon Light Green

Mask, yellow ornamented by six evenly spaced large round cinnamon brown throat spots, the outer two being partially covered at the base by cheek patches. *Cheek patches*, violet. *General body colour*, back, rump, breast, flanks and underparts, bright grass-green. 50% of normal body colour depth. *Markings*, on cheeks, back of head, neck and wings, cinnamon brown well defined on a yellow ground. *Tail*, long feathers dark blue with brown quill. *Feet and legs*, pinkish grey. *Eye*, black with a white iris.

Cinnamon Dark Green

As above but with a light laurel green body colour. *Tail*, long feathers darker in proportion.

Cinnamon Olive Green Pl. 19

As above but with a light olive green body colour. *Tail*, long feathers darker in proportion.

Cinnamon Grey Green Pl. 18

As above but with a pale grey-green body colour. *Tail*, long feathers of deep cinnamon shade.

Cinnamon Sky Blue

Mask, white ornamented by six evenly spaced large round cinnamon brown throat spots, the outer two being partially covered at the base by cheek patches. *Cheek patches*, violet. *General body colour*, back, rump, breast, flanks and underparts, pure sky blue. 50% of normal body colour depth. *Markings*, on cheeks, back of head, neck and wings, cinnamon brown on white ground. *Tail*, long feathers blue with brown quill. *Feet and legs*, pinkish grey. *Eye*, black with a white iris.

Cinnamon Cobalt

As above but with a pale cobalt body colour. *Tail*, long feathers as above but cobalt.

Cinnamon Mauve

As above but with a pale mauve body colour. *Tail*, long feathers as above but mauve.

Cinnamon Violet Cobalt

As above but with a pale violet body colour. *Tail*, long feathers of pale cinnamon shade.

Cinnamon Grey

The Cinnamon Grey conforms to the standard for Cinnamon Skyblue except in the following details: *Cheek patches*, grey. *General body colour*, grey, 50% of normal body colour depth. *Tail*, long feathers deep cinnamon brown. (It should be noted that there are light, medium and dark shades of Cinnamon Grey.)

Fallow Light Green Pl. 23

Mask, yellow ornamented by six evenly spaced large round brown throat spots, the outer two being partially covered at the base by cheek patches. *Cheek patches*, violet. *General body colour*, back, rump, breast, flanks and underparts, yellowish green. *Markings*, on cheeks, back of head, neck and wings, medium brown on a yellow ground. *Eye*, red or plum. *Tail*, long feathers bluish. *Feet and legs*, pinkish grey.

Fallow Dark Green

As above but with a dark yellowish laurel green body colour. *Tail*, long feathers darker in proportion.

Fallow Olive Green

As above but with a light mustard olive body colour. *Tail*, long feathers darker in proportion.

Fallow Grey Green

As above but with a dull mustard green body colour. *Tail*, long feathers darker in proportion.

Fallow Sky Blue

Mask, white ornamented by six evenly spaced large round brown throat spots, the outer two being partially covèred at the base by cheek patches. *Cheek patches*, violet. *General body colour*, back, rump, breast, flanks and underparts, pale sky blue. *Markings*, on cheeks, back of head, neck and wings, brown on a white ground. *Tail*, long feathers bluish grey. *Eye*, red or plum. *Feet and legs*, pinkish grey.

Fallow Cobalt Pl. 24

As above but with a warm pale cobalt body colour. *Tail*, long feathers darker in proportion.

Fallow Mauve

As above but with a pale mauve body colour of a pinkish tone. *Tail*, long feathers darker in proportion.

Fallow Violet Cobalt

As above but with a pale violet body colour. *Tail*, long feathers darker in proportion.

Fallow Grey

As above but with a pale grey body colour. *Cheek patches*, grey. *Tail*, long feathers darker in proportion. (It should be noted that there are light, medium and dark shades of Fallow Grey.)

NOTE. English and German forms of the Fallow are recognised; the German form having a white iris ring around the eye, the English form has none.

Lutino Pl. 25

Buttercup yellow throughout. *Eyes*, red with a white iris. *Tail*, long feathers and primaries whitish. *Feet and legs*, fleshy pink.

Albino Pl. 26

White throughout. *Eyes*, red with a white iris. *Feet and legs*, fleshy pink.

Opaline Light Green Pl. 27

Mask, buttercup yellow, ornamented by six evenly spaced large round black throat spots, the outer two being partially covered by the base of the cheek patches, the yellow of the mask should extend over back of head and merge into the general body colour at a point level with the butt of the wings where undulations should cease thus leaving a clear V effect between top of wings. *Cheek patches*, violet. *General body colour*, mantle (including V area or saddle) back, rump, breast, flanks and underparts bright grass green. *Markings on wings*, should be normal and symmetrical, black on a body colour ground with a suffused opalescent effect. *Tail*, dark blue. *Feet and legs*, blue/grey mottled. *Eye*, black with a white iris.

Opaline Dark Green

As above but with a dark laurel green body colour. *Tail*, long feathers darker in proportion.

Opaline Olive Green

As above but with an olive green body colour. *Tail*, long feathers darker in proportion.

Opaline Grey Green Pl. 28

As above but with a dull mustard green body colour. *Tail*, long feathers have light centre with black edging. *Cheek patches*, grey.

Opaline Sky Blue Pl. 29

As above but with a skyblue body colour and suffusion, and white mask instead of buttercup. *Tail*, long feathers have light centre with deep blue edging.

Opaline Cobalt

As above but with a cobalt body colour. *Tail*, long feathers darker in proportion.

Opaline Mauve

As above but with a mauve body colour. *Tail*, long feathers darker in proportion.

Opaline Violet Cobalt Pl. 30

As above but with a deep intense violet body colour. *Tail*, long feathers darker in proportion.

Opaline Grey

As above but with a solid grey body colour. *Cheek patches*, grey. *Tail*, long feathers have light centre with black edging.

Opaline Cinnamon Light Green

Mask, buttercup yellow, ornamented by six evenly spaced large round cinnamon brown throat spots, the outer two being partially covered by the base of the cheek patches, the yellow of the mask should extend over back of head and merge into the general body colour at a point level with the butt of the wings where undulations should cease thus leaving a clear V effect between top of wings. *Cheek patches*, violet.

General body colour, mantle (including V area or saddle) back, rump, breast, flanks and underparts bright grass green. 50% of normal body colour depth. *Markings on wings*, should be normal and symmetrical, cinnamon brown on a body colour ground with a suffused opalescent effect. *Tail*, long feathers dark blue with a brown quill. *Feet and legs*, pinkish grey. *Eye*, black with a white iris.

Opaline Cinnamon Dark Green Pl. 31

As above but with a dark laurel green body colour. 50% of normal body colour depth. *Tail*, long feathers darker in proportion.

Opaline Cinnamon Olive Green

As above but with a deep olive green body colour. 50% of normal body colour depth. *Tail*, long feathers darker in proportion.

Opaline Cinnamon Grey Green Pl. 32

The Opaline Cinnamon Grey Green conforms to the standard for Opaline Cinnamon Light Green except in the following details: *Cheek patches*, grey. *General body colour*, dull mustard green. 50% of normal body colour depth. *Tail*, long feathers deep cinnamon brown. (It should be noted that there are light, medium, and dark shades of Opaline Cinnamon Grey Green.)

Opaline Cinnamon Skyblue

Mask, white, ornamented by six evenly spaced large round cinnamon brown throat spots, the outer two being partially covered by the base of the cheek patches, the white of the mask should extend over back of the head and merge into the general body colour at a point level with the butt of the wings where undulations should cease thus leaving a clear V effect between top of wings. *Cheek patches*, violet. *General body colour*, mantle (including V area or saddle) back, rump, breast, flanks and underparts pure skyblue. 50% of normal body colour depth. *Markings on wings*, should be normal and symmetrical cinnamon brown on a body colour ground with a suffused opalescent effect. *Tail*, long feathers dark blue with a brown quill. *Feet and legs*, pinkish grey. *Eye*, black with a white iris.

Opaline Cinnamon Cobalt Pl. 33

As above but with a deep rich cobalt body colour. 50% of normal body colour depth. *Tail*, long feathers darker in proportion.

Opaline Cinnamon Mauve

As above but with a purplish mauve body colour with a tendency to a pinkish tone. *Tail*, long feathers darker in proportion.

Opaline Cinnamon Violet Cobalt

As above but with a deep intense violet body colour. 50% of normal body colour depth. *Tail*, long feathers have light centre with cinnamon edging.

Opaline Cinnamon Grey

The Opaline Cinnamon Grey conforms to the standard for Opaline Cinnamon Skyblue except in the following details: *Cheek patches*, grey. *General body colour*, grey. 50% of normal body colour depth. *Tail*, long feathers deep cinnamon brown. (It should be noted that there are light, medium and dark shades of Opaline Cinnamon Grey.)

Opaline Greywing Light Green

Mark, buttercup yellow, ornamented by six evenly spaced large round grey throat spots, the outer two being partially covered by the base of the cheek patches, the yellow of the mask should extend over the back of head and merge into the general body colour at a point level with the butt of the wings. *Cheek patches*, light violet. *General body colour*, mantle (including V area of saddle) back, rump, breast, flanks and underparts bright grass green, 50% of normal body colour depth. *Markings on wings*, should be normal and symmetrical light grey on a body colour ground with a suffused opalescent effect. *Tail*, long feathers grey with bluish tinge. *Feet and legs*, blue/grey mottled. *Eye*, black with a light iris.

Opaline Greywing Dark Green

As above but with a dark laurel green body colour. 50% of normal body colour depth. *Tail*, long feathers, darker in proportion.

Opaline Greywing Olive Green

As above but with a deep olive green body colour. 50% of normal body colour depth. *Tail*, long feathers, darker in proportion.

Opaline Greywing Skyblue

Mask, white ornamented by six evenly spaced large round grey throat spots, the outer two being partially covered by the base of the cheek patches, the white of the mask should extend over the back of the head and merge into the general body colour at a point level with the butt of the wings where undulations should cease thus leaving a clear V effect between top of wings. *Cheek patches*, light violet. *General body colour*, mantle (including V area or saddle) back, rump, breast, flanks and underparts pure skyblue, 50% of normal body colour depth. *Markings on wings*, should be normal and symmetrical light grey on a body colour ground with a suffused opalescent effect. *Tail*, long feathers grey with a bluish tinge. *Feet and legs*, blue/grey mottled. *Eye*, black with a white iris.

Opaline Greywing Cobalt

As above but with a rich cobalt body colour. 50% of normal body colour depth. *Tail*, long feathers, darker in proportion.

Opaline Greywing Mauve

As above but with a purplish mauve body colour. 50% of normal body colour depth. *Tail*, long feathers, darker in proportion.

Opaline Greywing Violet Cobalt

As above but with a deep intense violet body colour. 50% of normal body colour depth. *Tail*, long feathers, darker in proportion.

Opaline Greywing Grey

The Opaline Greywing Grey conforms to the standard for Opaline Greywing Skyblue except in the following details: *Cheek patches*, light grey. (It should be noted that there are light, medium and dark shades of Opaline Greywing Grey.)

Yellow-faced Pl. 38–43

All varieties in the Blue series mask, yellow only, otherwise exactly as corresponding normal variety.

Note. Yellow suffusion on wing butts and tail permissible.

Additional Visual Factors. When a bird carries any additional visual factor other than those given in the Standards, such birds must be exhibited in the Any Other Colour Class unless separate classes are provided. For example: if the schedule reads 'Opaline Cinnamon', then only the Opaline Cinnamon colours as laid down in the Standards are eligible for this class. If no class is provided they must be entered in the A.O.C. Class.

PIEDS

Recessive Pied Light Green Pl. 44

Mask, buttercup yellow. *Throat spots*, as the normal Light Green variety, may be present from one to full number. *Cheek patches*, violet, silvery white or a mixture of both. *General body colour*, irregular patches of clear buttercup yellow and bright grass green with the latter mainly on the lower chest, rump and underparts. *Wings*, black undulations or polka dot markings should not cover more than 15–20% of total area. All visible flight feathers should be clear yellow but odd dark flight feathers are not faults. *Cere*, fleshy pink. *Beak*, oranged coloured. *Feet and legs*, fleshy pink. *Eye*, dark without any light iris ring.

Recessive Pied Dark Green

As above but with a yellow and dark green body colour. *Tail*, long feathers; blue, yellow or a mixture of both.

Recessive Pied Olive Green

As above but with a yellow and olive green body colour. *Tail*, long feathers; blue, yellow or a mixture of both.

Recessive Pied Grey Green

As above but with yellow and grey-green body colour. *Cheek patches*, grey-blue or slate or a mixture of both. *Tail*, long feathers, grey black, yellow or a mixture of both. (It should be noted that there are light medium and dark shades of Recessive Pied Grey Green.

Recessive Pied Skyblue

Mask, white. *Throat spots*, as the normal skyblue variety, may be present from one to full number. *Cheek patches*, violet, silvery white or a mixture of both. *General body colour*, irregular patches of white and pure skyblue with the latter mainly on the lower chest, rump and underparts. *Wings*, black undulations or polka dot markings should not cover more than 15–20% of total area. All visible flight feathers should be white but odd dark flight feathers are not faults. *Cere*, fleshy pink. *Beak*, orange coloured. *Feet and legs*, fleshy pink. *Eye*, dark without any light iris ring.

Recessive Pied Cobalt Pl. 45

As above but with a white and cobalt body colour. *Tail*, long feathers; blue, white or a mixture of both.

Recessive Pied Mauve

As above but with a white and mauve body colour. *Tail*, long feathers; blue, white or a mixture of both.

Recessive Pied Violet Cobalt

As above but with a white and violet body colour. *Tail*, long feathers; blue, white or a mixture of both.

Recessive Pied Grey

As above but with a white and grey body colour. *Cheek patches*, grey-blue or slate or a mixture of both. *Tail*, long feathers, grey black, white or a mixture of both. (It should be noted that there are light medium and dark shades of Recessive Light Grey.)

NOTE. Recessive Pied also known as Danish Recessive Pied.

Dominant Pied Light Green Pl. 49

Mask, buttercup yellow, ornamented by six evenly spaced large round black throat spots, the outer two being partially covered by the base of the cheek patches. *Cheek patches*, violet. *General body colour*, bright grass green as the normal variety but broken with irregular patches of clear buttercup yellow or with a clear yellow band approximately half an inch wide around its middle just above the thighs. *Head patch*, at back of head should be clear yellow and is optional. *Wings*, colour and markings as the normal Light Green but having irregular patches of clear buttercup yellow or with part of the wing edges up to shoulder clear yellow on an otherwise normally marked wing. Wing markings may be grizzled in appearance, all visible flight feathers should be clear yellow but odd dark flight feathers are not faults. *Tail*, long feathers may be clear yellow, marked or dark blue. *Cere*, similar to that of the normal variety or a mixture of normal colour and fleshy pink. *Feet and legs*, blue/grey mottled, fleshy pink or a mixture of both. *Eye*, black with a white iris.

Dominant Pied Dark Green

As above but with general body colour as for normal dark green. *Tail*, long feathers; blue, yellow or a mixture of both.

Dominant Pied Olive Green

As above but with general body colour as for normal olive green. *Tail*, long feathers; blue, yellow or a mixture of both.

Dominant Pied Skyblue

Mask, white ornamented by six evenly spaced large round black throat spots, the outer two being partially covered by the base of the cheek patches. *Cheek patches*, violet. *General body colour*, pure skyblue as the normal variety but broken with irregular patches of clear white or with a clear white band approximately half an inch wide around its middle just above the thighs. *Head patch*, at back of head should be clear white and is optional. *Wings*, colour and markings as the normal Skyblue but having irregular patches of clear white, or with part of the wing edges up to shoulder clear white on an otherwise normally marked wing. Wing markings may be grizzled in appearance, all visible flight feathers should be clear white but odd dark flight feathers are not faults. *Tail*, long feathers may be clear white, marked or dark blue. *Cere*, similar to that of the normal variety or a mixture of normal colour and fleshy pink. *Feet and legs*, blue/grey mottled fleshy pink or a mixture of both. *Eye*, black with a white iris.

Dominant Pied Cobalt

As above but with general body colour as for normal cobalt. *Tail*, long feathers, blue, white or a mixture of both.

Dominant Pied Mauve

As above but with general body colour as for normal mauve. *Tail*, long feathers, blue, white or a mixture of both.

Dominant Pied Violet Cobalt

As above but with general body colour as for normal violets. *Tail*, long feathers, blue, white or a mixture of both.

Dominant Pied Grey

As above but with general body colour as for normal grey. *Cheek patches*, grey-blue or slate. *Tail*, long feathers; black, white or a mixture of both.

Clearflight Light Green Pl. 57

Mask, buttercup yellow, ornamented by six evenly spaced large round black throat spots, the outer two being partially covered by the base of the cheek patches. *Cheek patches*, violet. *General body colour*, as the normal Light Green with the exception of one small patch approximately half an inch by five-eighths inch of clear buttercup yellow at the back of the head. Slight collar or extension of bib, while undesirable, will not penalize. *Wings*, colour and markings as the normal Light Green but with seven visible flight feathers of clear yellow. Dark flights constitute a fault. *Tail*, long feathers clear yellow, dark tail feathers are a fault. *Cere*, as the normal. *Feet and legs*, blue/grey mottled or fleshy pink. *Eye*, black with a white iris.

Clearflight Dark Green

As above but with general body colour as for normal Dark Green.

Clearflight Olive Green

As above but with general body colour as for normal Olive Green.

Clearflight Grey Green

As above but with general body colour as for normal Grey Green. *Cheek patches*, grey. There are light, medium and dark shades of clearflight Grey Green.

Clearflight Skyblue

Mask, white ornamented by six evenly spaced large round black throat spots, the outer two being partially covered by the base of the cheek patches. *Cheek patches*, violet. *General body colour*, as the normal

Skyblue with the exception of one small patch approximately half an inch by five eighths inch of pure white at the back of the head. Slight collar or extension of bib while undesirable will not penalize. *Wings*, colour and markings as the normal Skyblue but with seven visible pure white flight feathers. Dark flights constitute a fault. *Tail*, long feathers pure white, dark tail feathers are a fault. *Cere*, as the normal. *Feet and legs*, blue/grey mottled or fleshy pink. *Eye*, black with a white iris.

Clearflight Cobalt

As above but with general body colour as for normal cobalt. *Tail*, white. Marked or dark tail feathers constitute a fault.

Clearflight Mauve

As above but with general body colour as for normal mauve. *Tail*, white. Marked or dark tail feathers constitute a fault.

Clearflight Violet Cobalt

As above but with general body colour as normal violet. *Tail*, white. Marked or dark tail feathers constitute a fault.

Clearflight Grey

As above but with general body colour as for normal grey. *Cheek patches*, grey. *Tail*, white. Marked or dark tail feathers constitute a fault. There are light, medium and dark shades of Clearflight Grey.

Dark-eyed Clear Yellow Pl. 59

Cheek patches, silvery white. *General body colour*, pure yellow throughout and free from any green suffusion or odd green feathers. *Wings*, pure yellow throughout free from green suffusion and black or grizzled tickings. Flight feathers paler yellow than rump. *Tail*, as flight feathers. *Eyes*, dark or deep plum red without any white rings. *Beak*, orange-coloured. *Feet and legs*, flesh-coloured. *Cere*, fleshy pink. *Eye*, dark without any light iris ring.

NOTE. The actual depth of body colour varies according to genetical make-up, i.e., whether light, dark or olive green, etc.

Dark-eyed Clear White

As above but with white body colour and free from any blue suffusion or odd blue feathers. *Flights and tail*, white. *Cere*, fleshy pink. *Eye*, dark without any light iris ring.

A Yellow-faced form of Dark-eyed Clear is also recognized.

NOTE. A dominant form is also recognised having normal cere, beak, feet and legs which may be exhibited with the above mentioned types of Dark-eyed Clear Whites/Yellows where separate classes are scheduled for this variety. A Yellow-faced form of Dark-eyed Clear White is also recognised but these should only be exhibited in Dark-eyed classes.

Lacewing Yellow

Mask, yellow, ornamented by six evenly spaced large round cinnamon brown throat spots, the outer two being partially covered by the base of the cheek patches. *Cheek patches*, pale violet. *General body colour*, back, rump, breast, flanks and underparts, yellow. *Markings*, on cheeks, back of head, neck, mantle and wings, cinnamon brown on a yellow ground. *Tail*, long feathers cinnamon brown. *Feet and legs*, fleshy pink. *Eye*, red with a white iris.

NOTE. Intensity of body colour will vary in depth according to the normal counterpart being masked, i.e. the richest body colour is carried by the Lacewing Olive Green and the lightest by the Lacewing Light Green.

Lacewing White

As above but with general body colour white. *Markings*, cinnamon brown on a white ground.

NOTE. The shade of white of the body colour varies only slightly in tone according to the normal counterpart being masked. A Yellow-face form is recognised. Where no classes are scheduled Lacewings should be exhibited in Any Other Colour classes.

The Crested Varieties

Circular crest, this should be a flat round crest with the feathers radiating from the centre of the head.

Half-circular crest, this should be a half circle of feathers falling or raised in a fringe above the cere.

Tufted crest, this should be an upright crest of feathers up to three eighths of an inch high rising just above the cere. The crested character can be combined visibly with all the other colours and varieties aforementioned in these standards and the standard should be exactly as written for each colour and variety plus either a Circular, Half-circular or Tufted Crest as described above.

Spangle Light Green

Mask, yellow of even tone ornamented on each side of the throat with three clearly defined black spots with yellow centres. *Cheek patches*, violet with silvery white feathers appearing on each cheek patch. *Body colour*, back, rump, breasts, flanks and underparts bright light green of a solid and even shade throughout. *Wing markings*, yellow with all feathers edged with black. *Tail*, yellow or yellow edged with black.

Spangle Dark Green

As above but body colour dark laurel green. *Tail*, yellow or yellow edged with black.

Spangle Olive

As above but body colour deep olive green. *Tail*, yellow or yellow edged with black.

Spangle Grey Green

This variety conforms to the standard of each of the green varieties except the *Cheek patches*, which are grey. *Body colour*, of a solid and even shade of mustard green. *Tail*, yellow or yellow edged with black.

Spangle Skyblue

Mask, clear white ornamented on each side of the throat with three clearly defined black throat spots with white centres of each black spot. *Cheek patches*, violet with silvery white feathers appearing on each cheek patch. *Body colour*, back, rump, breast, flanks and underparts pure skyblue of a solid and even shade throughout. *Wing markings*, white with all feathers edged with black. *Tail*, white or white edged with black.

Spangle Cobalt

As above but body colour rich deep cobalt. *Tail*, white or white edged with black.

Spangle Mauve

As above but body colour purplish mauve. *Tail*, white or white edged with black.

Spangle Grey

This variety conforms to the standards of each of the blue varieties except the: *Cheek patches*, which are blue grey or slate. *Body colour*, of a solid grey. *Tail*, white or white edged with black.

NOTE. *The spangle variety, Spangle Light Green etc.* The above are the colour standards of the Australian National Budgerigar Council for the normal Green and Blue series Spangle variety, it is recognised that the Spangle character can be combined visibly with most other varieties. With the kind permission of the Australian National Budgerigar Council the Budgerigar Society has adopted the above standards for the Spangle for the time being; the position will be reviewed when this new mutation becomes more widespread and experience is gained of its breeding behaviour.

THE COLOUR PLATES

These illustrations are examples of each group of Budgerigars, although not all colour shades and variations are included.

If the chapters on the groups are read in conjunction with the Colour Standards immediately preceding the illustrations (pages 17 to 31), the reader should be able to recognize all the different colour combinations.

References to the plate numbers of the colour pages are given in the text, and in the index.

Light Green

Dark Green

Olive Green

Grey Green

Light Yellow

Olive Yellow

Sky Blue

Cobalt

Mauve

Violet Cobalt (Visual Violet)

Light Grey

White Sky Blue (Dark Suffusion)

14 Light Yellow

Yellow-wing
Light Green

Greywing Light Green

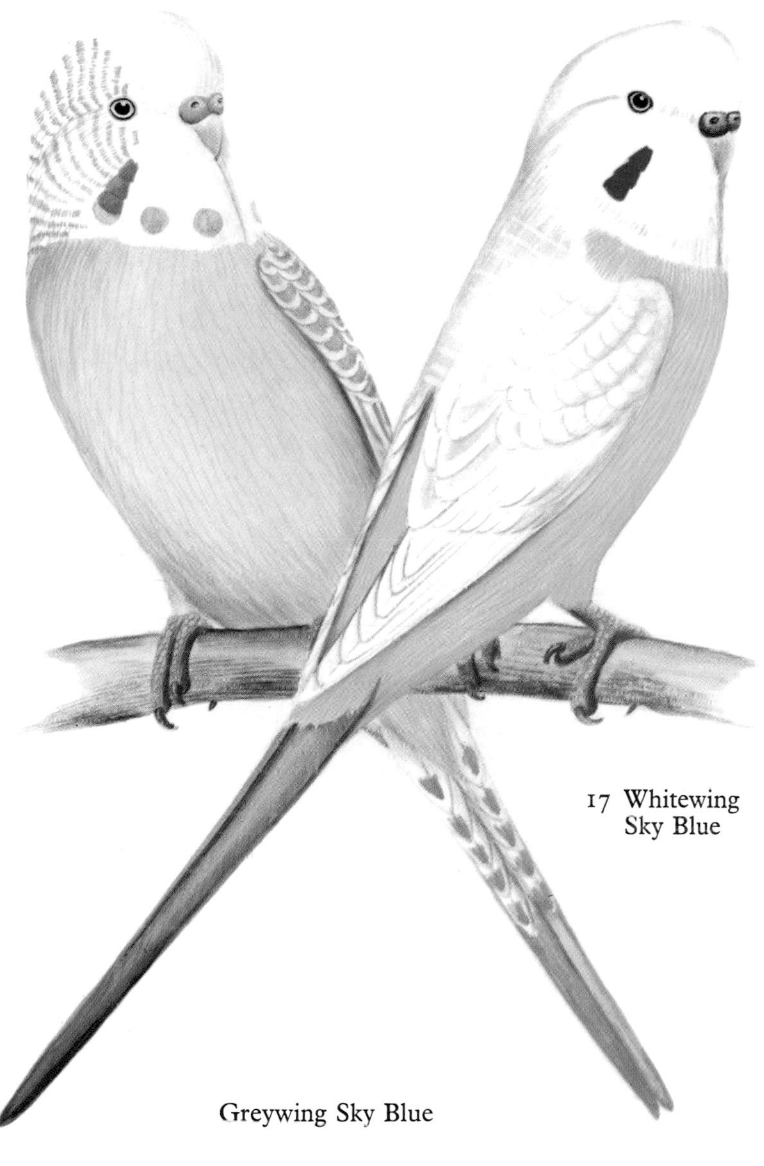

17 Whitewing Sky Blue

Greywing Sky Blue

19 Cinnamon Dark Gre

Cinnamon Grey
Green

Cinnamon Greywing Dark Green

Yellow-wing Dark Green

Whitewing Violet Cobalt

Fallow Light Green

Fallow Cobalt

Lutino (Red-eyed Clear Yellow)

Albino (Red-eyed Clear White)

Opaline Light Green

Opaline Grey Green

Opaline Sky Blue

Opaline Violet Cobalt

Opaline Cinnamon Dark Green

Opaline Cinnamon Grey Green

Opaline Cinnamon Cobalt

Opaline Cinnamon Grey

Opaline Yellow-wing Dark Green

White-flighted Opaline Cobalt

Australian White-flighted Sky Blue

Yellow-faced Sky Blue

Yellow-faced Greywing Cobalt

Yellow-faced Fallow Sky Blue

Yellow-faced Cinnamon Grey

Yellow-faced Cinnamon Greywing Cobalt

Yellow-faced Opaline Mauve

Recessive Pied Light Green

Recessive Pied Cobalt

Recessive Pied Cinnamon Violet Cobalt

Recessive Pied Opaline Dark Green

Recessive Pied Yellow-faced Sky Blue

Dominant Pied
Light Green

Dominant Pied Sky Blue

Dominant Pied Greywing Cobalt

Dominant Pied Opaline Dark Green

Australian Dominant Banded Pied Light Green

Australian Dominant Banded Pied Cobalt

Australian Dominant Banded Pied Light Grey

Australian Dominant Banded Pied Opaline
Cinnamon Dark Green

Yellow-flighted Light Green

Australian Yellow-flighted Light Green

Dark-eyed Clear Yellow

Slate Sky Blue

Violet Dark Green

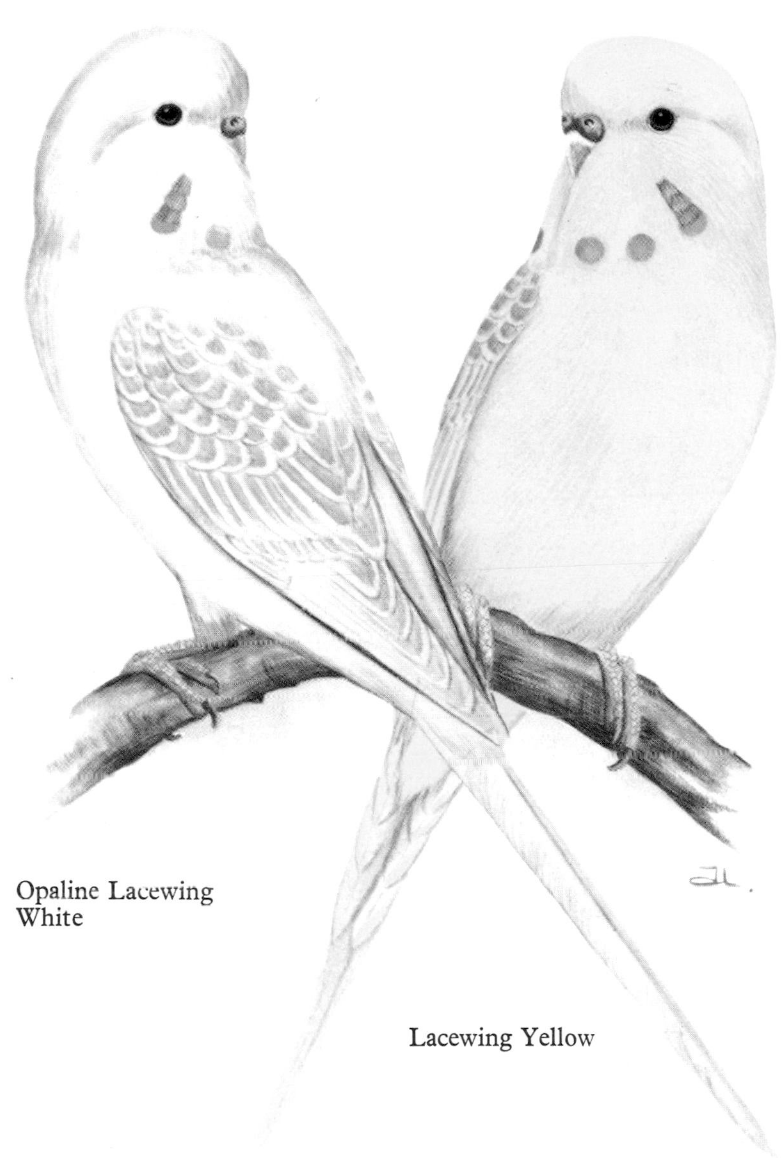
Opaline Lacewing
White
Lacewing Yellow

Yellow-faced Opaline Whitewing Cobalt (Rainbow)

Yellow-faced Opaline Whitewing Sky Blue (Rainbow)

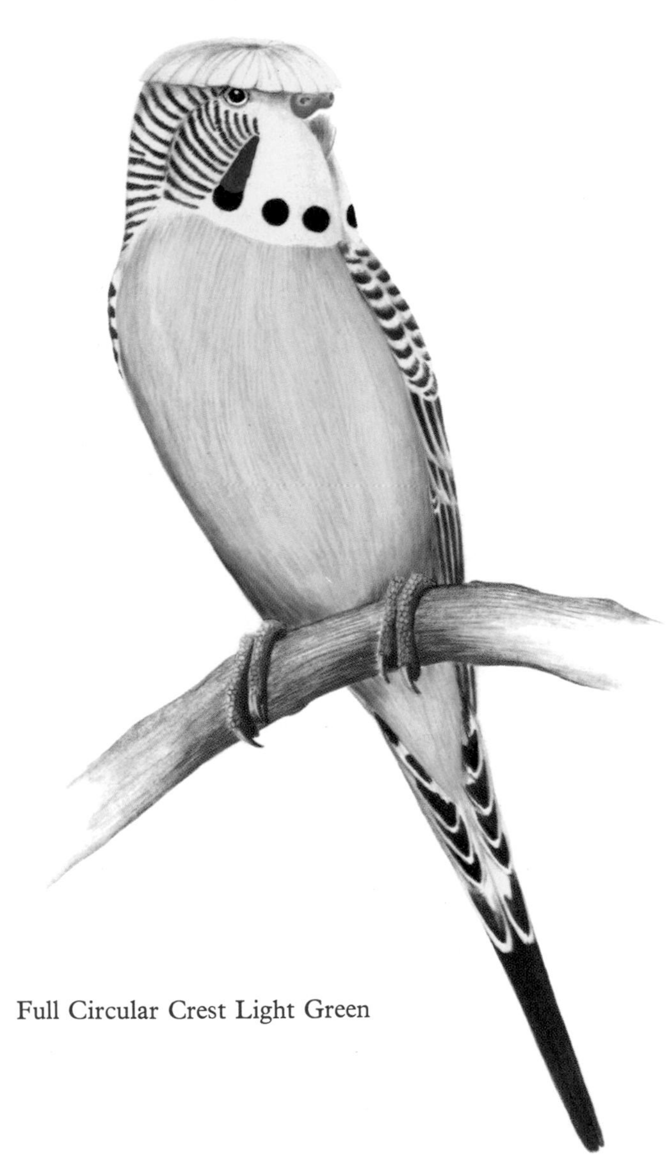

Full Circular Crest Light Green

Half-circular Crest Sky Blue

Tufted Crest Cinnamon Light Grey

4. ACCOMMODATION IN CAGES AND AVIARIES

If we want to keep birds we should love them, and so win their confidence. The proper care of domestic birds demands on the part of their owners certain sacrifices of both time and money. Birds so treated will never fail to respond to any efforts we may make for their care and comfort. They will not only provide us with the opportunity of studying their habits in our homes, but their antics will also prove a constant source of delight and entertainment for us and our children.

If a Budgerigar is accustomed to human company, it may be easy to domesticate, and a pair of the birds may breed if the accommodation is suitable. All the same, the bird does show some peculiarities that detract from its desirability as a guest in our living-room. There certainly are a number of birds that, on account of their wonderful colours, their charming disposition and their gentle, melodious song, are an adornment to any cage or living-room. Budgerigars, however, never belie their parrot descent, and if a number of them get together they are apt to make such a noise as to make conversation or listening to the radio impracticable. As a rule, they will react promptly to any sound. As soon as they hear human voices they will start a lively and far from discreet conversation of their own; while music will only serve to stimulate their activities.

Personally, I prefer to keep no more than two pairs in my living-room. If a bird is to learn to talk, it should, of course, be kept in the living-room. A lone Budgerigar will usually conceive a deep and lasting affection for its owner and its owner's family and will expect their attention and caresses in return. Two Budgies are, as a rule, models of mutual fondness and affection, and in many countries popular appreciation of their behaviour has resulted in the use of the expression 'They're like two budgies!' to describe young people too much in love to hide their feelings.

If, however, there are small children or babies in a family, I would not advise the keeping of Budgies, or for that matter any other birds, in the room where they live or play all day. Birds will usually shed tiny feathers which are liable to find their way into every nook and cranny of the room they inhabit and thus render it particularly unhealthy for little children. The bedroom, too, should not be used to house cage birds.

Feathers, however, will not find their way out of the glass walls of a cage except during the weekly cleaning. If, up till now, I had stressed the disadvantages and pointed out the dangers of keeping Budgerigar's I am left with the agreeable task of describing their many advantages, which obviously account for their great popularity. Their appeal lies not only in their vivaciousness, docility, playfulness and acrobatics, but also in their affection, their beautiful undulated markings and the endless array of colours they show. These qualities combined with their elegant and slender appearance make them irresistible.

Although this book is largely concerned with colour variability and how to achieve colour variation, it would be failing in its duty if it did not give some hints regarding the hobby in general and the problem of accommodation in particular.

In a preceding chapter, we learned something of the Budgerigar's way of life in its natural habitat in Australia; this knowledge may help the reader to solve some of the more difficult accommodation problems.

We should remember that, in their natural state, Budgerigars live in colonies. They change their habitats in flocks, they breed in close company and, in general, their life is governed by an outstanding sense of companionship.

They have certainly learned to adapt themselves to the changes brought about by their life among civilized people. Nevertheless, they have never lost certain characteristics of their mode of life in the wild state. It is not at all unusual for a pair of Budgerigars, kept by themselves in a roomy cage, to refuse to breed, even though the cage be well-furnished and provided with excellent nesting boxes, and despite the care given to their well-being. Such birds may still feel lonely. But if a few more birds are added to keep them company for the time being, and another nesting box or two installed, thus laying the foundations for their instinctive gregarious life, the birds will almost certainly start breeding at once, unless they are too old or suffer from some physical handicap which prevents them.

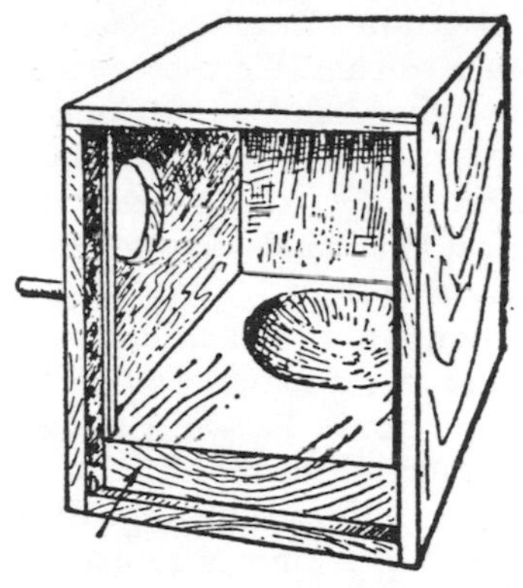

Box type of nest box
This will have either a slide or hinged door for easy inspection

The habit of breeding in hollows seems to be ineradicable. As far as I know, no Budgerigar ever bred in an open box. The shelter of nesting boxes is still indispensable to the success of a clutch. Nesting material, on the other hand, is still as superfluous as it was in Australia. Even if we provide it in abundance, the Budgerigars never have any use for it. Occasionally they will allow material put ready for use in the nesting box to remain where it is, just digging a little hole to receive the eggs, but as a rule the hen will thoroughly clean the box and throw out all the shavings, twigs or other bits of material before getting down to her task.

The natural bottom of a hole in a tree is concave, and although a Budgerigar will put up with a level bottom, it is always better to hollow out the bottom sufficiently for the eggs to remain close together, for a bird as active and alert as a Budgerigar may easily cause the eggs to scatter. Unless the hen puts them together again, we may later find only half-hatched eggs.

I always recommend the provision of poplar or birch logs to anyone wishing to have his Budgerigars breed in a metal or glass cage in his living-room. They please the eye and are more natural than any other breeding appliances, and an occasional inspection of the nest will not present any difficulty if they are fixed in a favourable position. Apart from this, they are not very expensive and, as a rule, will last for years. Moreover, they are decidedly easy to clean, despite popular belief. Budgerigars love gnawing and are certain to destroy any live plant or other vegetation placed in a metal or glass cage to shelter them. Instead it is the practice to paint the back wall of the cage. Against such a background, too, the birch logs will look better than any nesting boxes, however practical some of them may be. The Budgerigars will invariably alight on the bark of these logs and start to peck at them, clinging to them in all kinds of attitudes, even upside down, and so provide a fascinating sight.

When breeding is done in a bird room or in open-air flight instead of in the living-room, then, of course, the practical nesting boxes, which are easy to handle, are quite appropriate. They may be fixed on either the inside or the outside of the cages, the latter method making for quick and easy inspection of the nest. Self-made nesting boxes are, of course, somewhat cheaper. Budgerigars are not very exacting as regards accommodation and any roomy metal or glass cage may be made to serve. A canary cage, however, will not do, as it is usually too small for the purpose. A canary may be content to spend much of its time singing, but a Budgerigar needs climbing space and room for flight. If an old cage is used it will have to be thoroughly cleaned, and if any copper parts of it are accessible to the birds' beaks any traces of verdigris will have to be removed with the utmost care. Budgerigars are liable to pick or gnaw at everything and verdigris may well prove

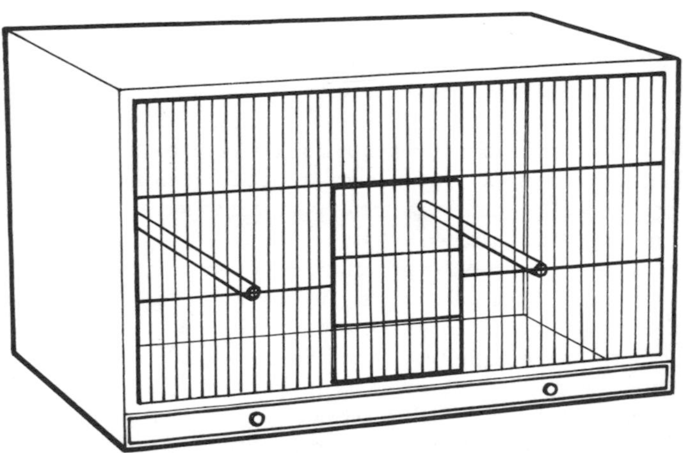

Breeding cage suitable for single pair of Budgerigars

to be fatal to them. Fortunately copper cages are no longer produced and a chromium-plated cage is no danger.

A wooden cage with bars may be made to do as well, but the capacity for picking and gnawing, which characterizes the hen even more than the cocks, will damage the woodwork considerably and soon turn the cage into an eyesore.

A glass cage with a glass front, glass sides and a hardboard back, whether the latter be rustically painted or not, always has considerable advantages over the wood or metal variety. When flying in a glass cage the birds will not fling feathers, sand and empty seed husks into the room. That is why we always provide the other varieties of cage with a 4 in. (10 cm) glass strip round the bottom, which will at least afford some protection.

The Budgerigar's passion for picking and gnawing will keep us perpetually on the look-out for a counter measure. By hanging up some fresh twigs in the cage we usually keep them from wreaking too much damage. Apart from this, gnawing at fresh twigs, especially willow and fruit tree twigs with young buds on them, is good for the bird's health. If the cage is painted on the inside care must be taken that no red lead or lead-white paint is used, as a bird swallowing some of this poison may die.

When furnishing the accommodation with the usual appliances, we should allow enough space for exercise so that the birds may fly about freely. To that end perches should be fixed as high and as near to the side as possible. These perches, by the way, have to be of freshly cut wood, if possible, and they should vary in width. Drinking or feeding appliances should never, of course, be fixed beneath them nor should any other perches be fixed there, as any birds sitting under a perch are liable to be soiled by the birds sitting over them. A Budgerigar will never make for a nesting box to get its night's sleep: it will always seek the highest perch. By the same token, the birds will always try to take possession of the highest nesting boxes—often a subject of heated contests between the hens, therefore nesting boxes should be fixed as near as possible at the same height.

Accommodation for Budgerigars should provide for feeding and drinking appliances fixed outside the cage. Such appliances will be easy to fill and clean and they do not run the risk of being dirtied.

Although a bathing appliance is superfluous since a Budgerigar

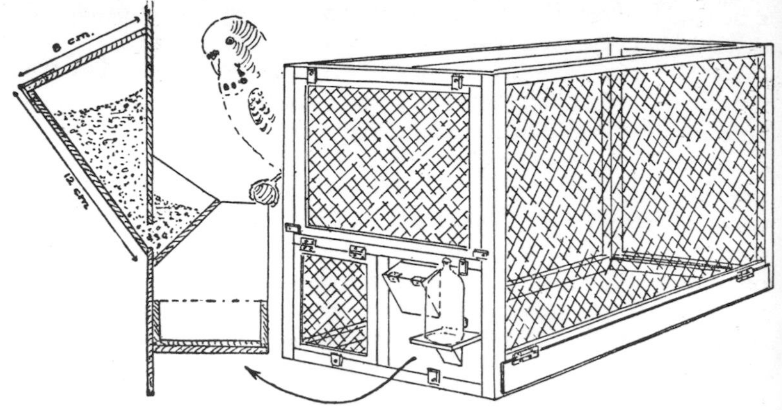

Feeding and drinking appliance fixed outside the cage

will rarely use it, such an appliance may be used for providing drinking facilities, and many a fancier will fix one to the outside of a cage.

Food and water should always be within easy reach, a perch at the right distance in front of food and water receptacles should also be provided. The fact that the birds rarely take a bath does not imply they are afraid of water. On the contrary, Budgerigars relish a real shower and find great fun in frolicking through a rain-soaked shrubbery. In order to meet this need in the living-room, we may safely treat them with a rose spray now and then. The water used should be kept at the ordinary room temperature. If the birds are kept in a glass cage or an aviary, a bundle of soaking wet grass may be hung in it now and again and will be much appreciated.

The place where the metal or glass cage is kept is, of course, of great importance to the birds' well-being. A site should be chosen in the full light of day, i.e. as near to a window as possible. If the cage is put in the rear of the room, well away from daylight, the birds may become nervous and easily frightened. When we stand near a cage our bodies may throw a shadow on it and frighten the birds. But when the cage is standing by the window the birds will be much less aware of our approach from another part of the room.

Although we should never put the cage directly in front of a window facing south in the full glare of the sun all day without giving the bird a chance to find a spot sheltered from the sun, we have to remember that the birds should enjoy the light of the sun for at least some time every day. If, nevertheless, there is no alternative but to place the cage in front of a window facing south, it is advisable that part of it should be covered so as to shelter them from the full glare. Many people do not trouble at first to instal climbing appliances, wooden rocking rings and swings in the cage, but experience shows the birds become extremely happy when given such contrivances. This gymnastic equipment is usually in continuous use all day and helps to keep them on the move and so enjoy good health. Swings and rocking rings are useful and beneficial, but dwarfs and other knick-knacks are best left out of the cage.

If plants are considered necessary they should adorn the outside of the cage, i.e. some hanging plants on the top and a few climbers on the sides. If the plants are placed beyond the birds' reach of the beaks, a green setting may look extremely attractive.

Metal or glass cages will have to be cleaned regularly and it is advisable to keep this in mind from the start. The floor should be furnished with a drawer that can be removed in a single movement. It is not necessary to change the sand on the floor (well-washed river sand or the excellent shell-sand sold in special packings) every time, but the excreta and the seed husks must be removed. In order to do this, the sand should be passed through a sieve specially set aside for the purpose, and a supply of fresh sand added. The drawer may then be pushed back into the cage.

You will notice that the birds remove the husk from every grain of seed they pick up, but they have no teeth to grind the grain itself. This is done in the stomach, and to help the process along the birds will also swallow little bits of grit which, of course, are of great help in the process. The need of lime is not the only reason for giving the birds grit and ground shells. Feeding and drinking vessels are obtainable in many varieties, and I propose to treat these important appliances in some detail. First of all, I should stress the paramount need for absolute cleanliness. The birds' water supply needs renewing every day. A daily review of the food supply, on the other hand, is just as necessary and when we inspect this we should, in the interests of cleanliness, blow away the husks that always gather on top of the seed. An adequate supply of food is indispensable at all times. A

Budgerigar cannot go without food for a long, or even a comparatively short, time and negligence in this respect is certain to lead to losses.

When keeping more than one pair of birds particular attention has to be paid to the number of nesting boxes. Two pairs need at least three, three pairs four or five, but even when keeping only a single pair the provision of two nesting boxes is recommended. It is an indisputable fact that the Budgerigar likes to pick and choose and, for reasons unknown, will occasionally refuse to use a box provided in what is considered a suitable spot. If two boxes are provided the birds will invariably carry out a minute inspection before making a definite choice. When the choice is made and the eggs are laid it is advisable, even though not strictly necessary, to remove the other box, as once in a while the hen will lay her eggs in both boxes, a practice that of course, will lead to nothing.

In the chapter on diseases, I shall revert to the moult although, naturally, the moult is not a disease. Nevertheless, the moult will make the bird look and behave in such a manner that the layman might think that his pet is in a bad way. The owner will then look up the chapter on diseases to find out what might be the matter with the bird. That is why the chapter includes the treatment the birds need in those circumstances. However, as we are now chiefly concerned with birds kept in the living-room, I have a few remarks to make in this connection.

The moult is very far from being the same for all Budgerigars, some taking as long as seven weeks to get the business over and done with. Occasionally the moult will proceed irregularly, piece by piece. It is in the nature of things that, during the moult, the birds are more sensitive than usual. As a rule living-room birds will have less stamina than those used to living in the open all the summer and frequently all the winter as well. Hence the former are particularly sensitive to cold when moulting. Now if we consider the fact that, during the moulting period, part of the food the little body takes to itself will be used for the production of nutriment for the new feathers, we shall not find it hard to understand that, at this stage, extra nourishment in the shape of a few drops of cod liver oil will come in very handy. Moults progressing without a hitch, i.e. quickly running their entire course, should find us even more on our guard against colds and draughts than others. As a rule, the moult may take place in or about the month of October. The moult will be sudden or gradual according to the weather. A sudden change from warmth to cold or vice-versa often provokes a partial moult. This is why so many birds coming from a show where, as a rule, it is warmer than in the open air or bird room, sometimes begin to moult upon their return.

I now want to devote a little space to various kinds of aviaries specially suitable for the accommodation of Budgerigars. There is, of course, a wide selection open to those who want to provide accommodation to give effect to their own pet ideas. My intention, however, is to outline a model of an aviary suited to the requirements of fanciers specializing in breeding. Before the construction of the aviary is discussed a few words on the question of where to put it, however, would not be out of place. The space available for the establishment is, of course, of decisive importance. For our purposes we shall assume that the fancier possesses, at the back of his house, a room facing on a small garden. There is usually some shed or other in the garden and if this cannot be used for our hobby, we can nearly always build on to it. If we may use the shed for a bird room, or even if we may only use part of it, it will be quite a help. But at worst we may build the sleeping quarters on to one of the walls and then add the open-air flight. Naturally, the question which way the aviary should face is of importance. If we are obliged to have the sleeping quarters and the aviary facing north where the birds will not get a single ray of sun, we shall have to drop the idea altogether. But let us suppose that there is a shed in the rear of our garden and that we may use part of it for our sleeping quarters. And, while we are at it, let us suppose as well that the afternoon and evening sun will shine on our future aviary. By means of rush matting, wood or board, we then screen off the north side, and the sleeping quarters must be provided with a window as well as with a little door leading to the aviary.

If we do not provide the aviary with a cement floor, and wish to retain the garden soil in our base, we shall have to lay fine mesh wire netting 12 in. into the ground to keep out rats, mice and other predators.

If there is a spacious garden in the rear of the house we can choose a favourable spot, and by laying out flower beds, shrubbery and lawns, make our aviary part of a pleasant general display. To go into too much detail about it would divert us from our purpose.

Here the Flight has been built on to the end part of a shed

If we decide to build a combined aviary and bird room, we shall first have to consider what materials are needed and their cost. Even if we do the work ourselves the expense is often greater than it appeared to be at first. Sometimes the opportunity arises of buying demolition waste, such as old window frames, fences, doors, etc. Anybody possessing a little practical skill will be able to make such material go a long way, although the fancier resorting to this method of cutting down costs should be forewarned of the fact that when the work is carried out with such materials, it is apt to give more trouble and take more time. Personally, I would advise a cement floor for the bird room because it keeps out mice as a wooden floor is invariably gnawed through. As to the open-air flight, a cement floor is, of course, completely feasible for it, but it certainly spoils the general aspect of the establishment. If we want to do without it, while still protecting

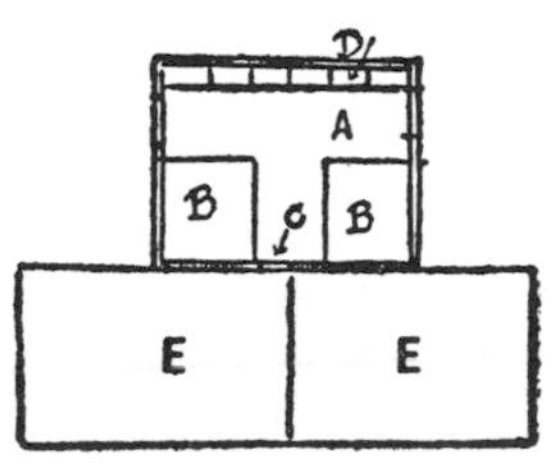

Plan of aviary opposite

A *Gangway*
B *Covered in flight*
C *Doors to outside flight*
D *Breeding cages*
E *Outdoor flights*

An interesting aviary. Note the small sliding doors leading from the house to the outside flight and the ventilation panel at the top

our aviary against mice, we always dig a trench of some 12–16 in. (30–40 cm) deep and some 12 in. (30 cm) wide around the aviary. We continue our wire netting to the bottom of the trench and fold a 12 in. (30 cm) strip outwards before filling in the earth. (See illustration.) In that way, the wire netting continues into the ground for 12 in. (30 cm), but also provides a horizontal protection of some 12 in. (30 cm) wide.

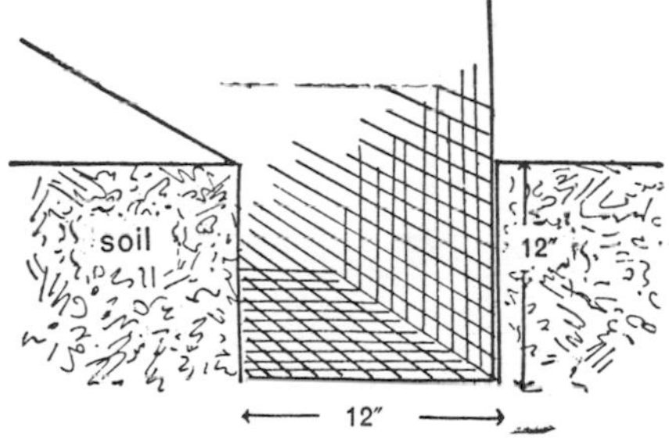

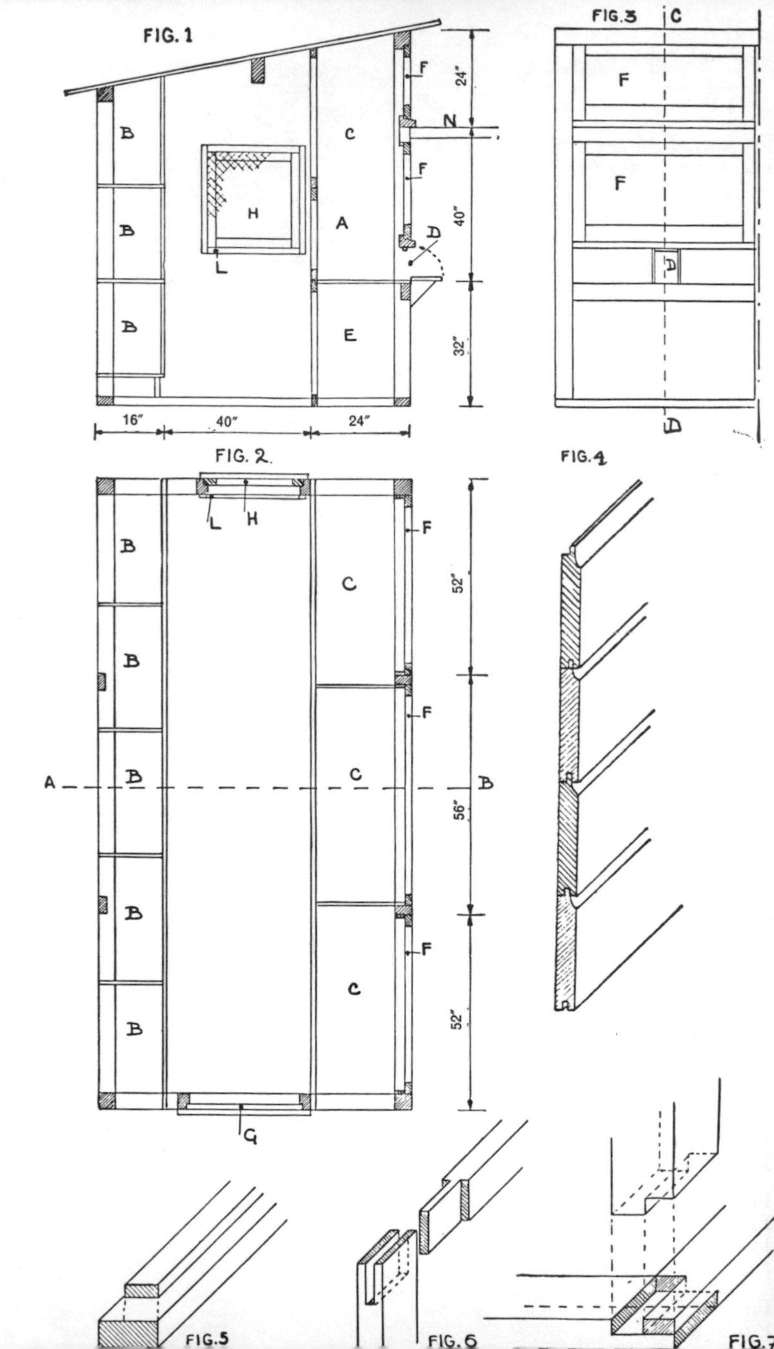

FIG. 1
B
B
B
H
L
C
A
E
F
F
N
D
24"
40"
32"
16"
40"
24"
FIG. 2.
L
H
B
B
B
B
B
C
C
C
F
F
F
A
B
52"
56"
52"
G
FIG. 3
C
F
F
D
D
FIG. 4
FIG. 5
FIG. 6
FIG. 7

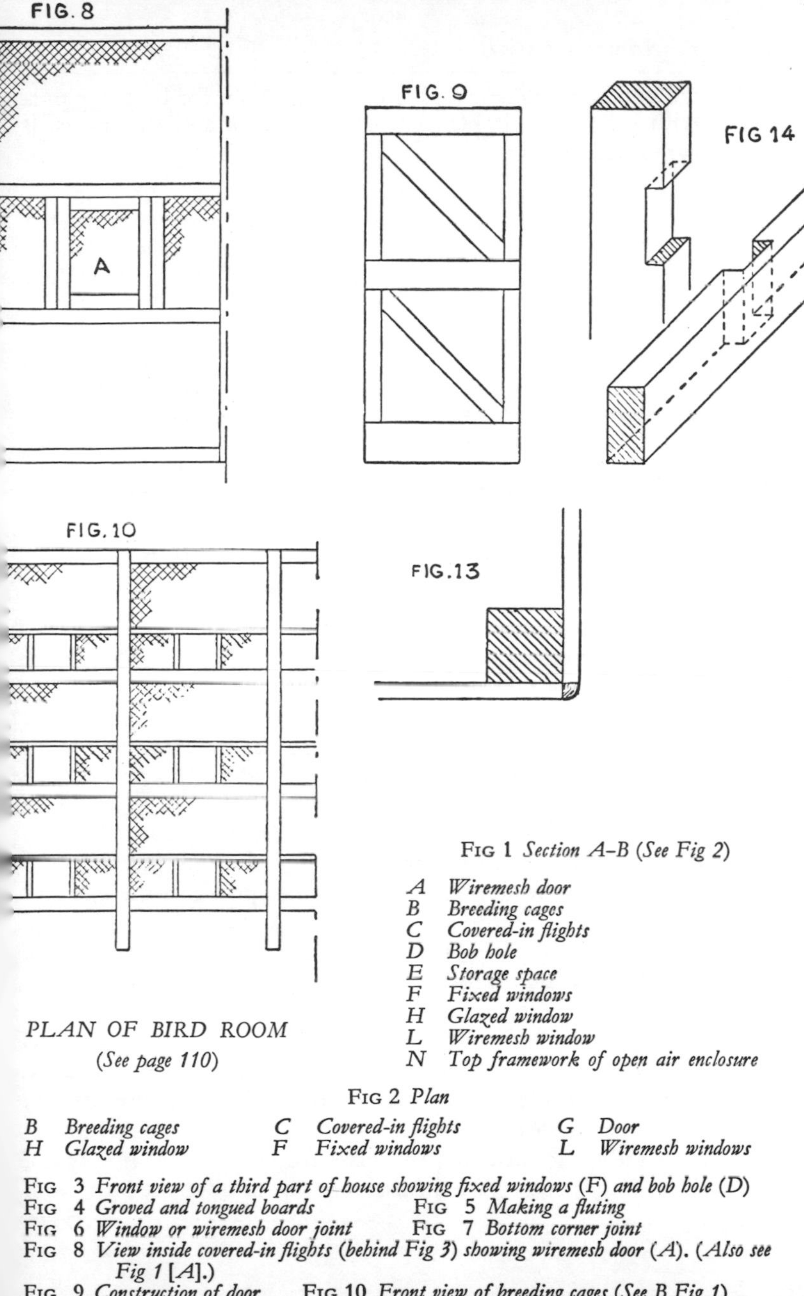

PLAN OF BIRD ROOM

(See page 110)

Fig 1 *Section A–B (See Fig 2)*

A *Wiremesh door*
B *Breeding cages*
C *Covered-in flights*
D *Bob hole*
E *Storage space*
F *Fixed windows*
H *Glazed window*
L *Wiremesh window*
N *Top framework of open air enclosure*

Fig 2 *Plan*

B *Breeding cages* *C* *Covered-in flights* *G* *Door*
H *Glazed window* *F* *Fixed windows* *L* *Wiremesh windows*

Fig 3 *Front view of a third part of house showing fixed windows* (F) *and bob hole* (D)
Fig 4 *Groved and tongued boards* Fig 5 *Making a fluting*
Fig 6 *Window or wiremesh door joint* Fig 7 *Bottom corner joint*
Fig 8 *View inside covered-in flights (behind Fig 3) showing wiremesh door* (*A*). (*Also see Fig 1* [*A*].)
Fig 9 *Construction of door* Fig 10 *Front view of breeding cages (See B Fig 1)*
Fig 11 *Joining vertical and horizontal framing* Fig 12 *Joining boards at corner*

On the previous pages is a plan of a bird room for breeding purposes with cages and flights. The specifications and the materials needed are listed below:

Corner posts and horizontal rafters	4 × 4 in. (10 × 10 cm)
Intermediate posts and all horizontal framings	2 × 4 in. (5 × 10 cm)
Intermediate rafters	2½ × 6 in. (6 × 15 cm)
Window framings	1½ × 3 in. (2·6 × 8 cm)
Boards, grooved, tongued and planed	1 × 6 in. (2·5 × 15 cm)
Boards, roof, grooved, tongued and planed	1 × 4 in. (2·5 × 10 cm)
Fluting laths for doors and windows	½ × 2½ in. (1·2 × 6 cm)
Fluting laths for glass	½ × 1 in. (1·2 × 2·5 cm)
Floor boards for covered-in flights and breeding cages	¾ × 4 in. (2 × 10 cm)
Partitions for covered-in flights and breeding cages	¾ × 4 in. (2 × 10 cm)
Inside fronts covered-in flights	1 × 3 in. (2·5 × 8 cm)
Fronts of breeding cages	½ × 3 in. (1·2 × 8 cm)
Wire netting doors and window frames	½ × 3 in. (1·2 × 8 cm)
Doors with hole in breeding cages	½ × 2 in. (1·2 × 5 cm)
Open-air flight:	
Corner posts and horizontal framing	2 × 3 in. (5 × 8 cm)
Doors	1 × 3 in. (2·5 × 8 cm)

The roof is covered with strong felt.

The floor consists of 12 in. sq. (30 cm sq.) cement tiles. The surface of the tiles is level with the bottom side of the bottom framing.

The space below the covered-in flights may be utilized as storage space; it also lends itself perfectly to use as accommodation for pheasants, quails and the like. If the space is used for this purpose the front is filled with another mesh wire window with entry and entry slide. It is advisable to construct the stone base in cement. This will allow of our putting in an occasional bolt with a nut to fasten the bottom framing to the stone base. The same applies to the open-air flight.

As to the breeding cages, the nesting boxes may be fixed to the outside of the breeding cages, i.e. to the front, so as to avoid having to reach into the cage every time.

The front should face south-west and have as many windows as possible. Each window should turn on hinges and open outwards. All glass must be protected by a screen of small mesh wire netting. This will keep the birds from flying through a broken pane. Moreover, birds are apt to mistake plain glass for an opening. If they do, they will fly into it and injure themselves. The door to the bird room should preferably be at the side. The front wall with all its windows is still provided with a few apertures in the top. We have to be able to open these, but in case we prefer to keep the windows closed they have to serve the birds as an entry into the open-air flight.

The nearer part of the open-air flight, i.e. the part adjoining the bird room, is covered with a strip of unbreakable or plate glass. In summer, the feeding table is put up in this covered part of the flight.

Materials for roofing can be welded asbestos or wood covered with bituminous felt; if the latter is used, it will have to be tarred regularly. There are several substitutes for bituminous felt but all of them are expensive.

The roof has to project a little over the rear side in order that the task of constructing a drain may be avoided. A similar projection in front is also very useful: it will prevent the rain from coming in.

Instead of ordinary mesh wire netting available almost everywhere in various widths, we may use the heavy, diamond-shaped mesh used in zoological gardens. This has the disadvantage of being very expensive, but if painted regularly it is almost indestructible. Our wire netting should be well galvanized and there should be no gaps in it.

Although tubes and angle irons certainly are the best and most durable materials for the open-air flight, I have often seen aviaries made of birch stems or peeled and painted tree branches, and I cannot deny that the effect was pleasing and picturesque. The Budgerigars will not damage them very much, and they will last for years. Tubing may be very useful but it certainly is completely inartistic. This may be neutralized, on the other hand, by having a pleasant growth of plants on top of the flight and a harmonious array of flowers and shrubbery in front of it. One should bear in mind that the aviary is part of the garden. That is why one should always be aware of the fact that the bird room, even if built out of demolition waste, should never turn into a ramshackle affair or detract from the beauty of the garden.

The question whether the inside of our bird room should be whitewashed, painted with white emulsion paint or treated with green solingum must be decided by the quantity of light falling into it. If, besides the front windows, we also have a skylight we should have no hesitation. The results will certainly not disappoint us when we perceive the birds in their variegated plumage against the pleasant green background. A whitewashed, or white emulsion painted wall is always unnaturally bleak and hard, but in a dark bird room it is indispensable.

The glass for the front windows should be double ply Vita glass if possible, as this glass will admit the ultra-violet rays of the sun indispensable to birds breeding in the nesting boxes of such a bird room. If, however, our birds are permitted to fly in and out of the bird room at will all the year round there is no need for Vita glass, and we may safely dispense with it.

It is advisable to provide the aviary with an entrance porch so as to prevent the possibility of escape.

I also recommend providing illumination for the bird room. In that way, we may shorten the long winter nights by having a 25-watt bulb burn there until 10 p.m. After that, a 5-watt bulb may be switched on. By means of this small second bulb, we may avoid any risk of trapping, at lights-out, a bird which has not found its sleeping place or a hen with chicks in the nest just having flown to the feeding table and now unable to return to the nesting box.

When, during the winter, windows are kept closed, ventilation becomes important. To effect this a small hinged panel should be fixed at the foot of the side wall and another at the top. The fresh air will enter by the lower panel and the spent air, being somewhat warmer, will rise and leave the room by the upper one. In this way, we get what is needed—circulation of air—but in a permanently closed indoor aviary, ventilation is a necessity.

There are, of course, many ways of building an aviary. The possibilities as regards exterior appearance and interior appointments are practically unlimited. Still, it must be our invariable purpose to keep out the cold north and east winds and to admit as much sun and light as possible.

As I have pointed out previously, it will be possible, more often than not, to transform old brick or wooden structures into ideal accommodation for our birds. Brick or double-walled wooden buildings always have one advantage over all others: the differences in temperature are liable to be appreciably smaller. Budgerigars can, however, stand a lot of cold, and we need not have excessive fears on this account.

In view of this, it is superfluous for any heating of the bird room as, in periods of extreme cold, we can introduce an infra-red radiator or a chicken lamp. Of course, one has to prevent the drinking water from freezing by keeping it on a tea-warmer or over a small floating wick or near an infra-red radiator or lighted bulb.

Green bushes or shrubs give very little pleasure in an aviary, as the Budgerigars ruin them quickly and I would advocate a grass plot covering flight area. It is also quite a good idea to sow some millet or oats in the aviary. Even if the plants will probably never bear seeds, the Budgerigars are certain to have enjoyed our efforts.

The rain must, of course, be able to enter that part of the aviary given over to grass, so we should never cover the entire open-air flight. Budgerigars love rain and are sure to frolic in the wet grass.

The provision of a few swings and rings should never be forgotten. They may seem to be nothing but superfluous toys, but experience shows that the birds will use them almost continuously, and I am convinced that all their gymnastic feats are a real benefit to health. Apart from this, it is a fascinating sight to see the birds practise their gymnastics on this equipment. A climbing pole on the other hand is appropriate to a cage and is out of place in an aviary.

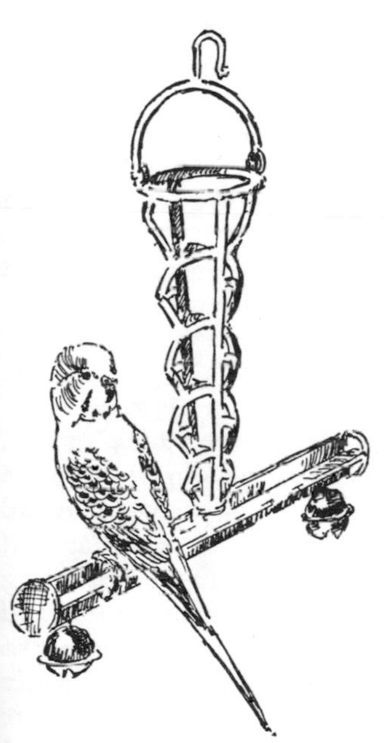

The perches should be firmly fixed near the top of the aviary, well apart, and they should be round, preferably of live wood, and their diameters ought to vary.

5. FEEDING

There are, of course, a number of seeds and cereals that, in themselves, are very good food for a Budgerigar, and I certainly shall not fail to discuss them. The Budgerigar earned its place in our households long enough ago for numerous firms to have marketed their own special seed mixtures. All these mixtures are available under the common name of Budgerigar Mixture.

Comparing several mixtures with one another, we are certain to identify several main ingredients all the mixtures have in common, but the fancier refusing to take any risks—and one actually should not take risks where livestock is concerned—buys Budgerigar Mixture in special packings vouching for a standard mixture of unchanging quality. All bird stores will offer such packings in a wide choice. To a fancier keeping only a few birds, the slight addition in price will certainly be no obstacle, and those having to cater for a larger number of birds may buy loose seeds and make their own blends.

It is advisable always to patronize a reputable bird seller who, in case of need, will gladly provide practical advice.

In Chapter 1 we saw how, in Australia, the Budgerigar lives on ripe grass seeds. Although we cannot provide such seeds over here, of course, we still have to ensure that the seed we give our birds is neither old nor stale. The value of the seed is dependent on its germinal force, and the following is an excellent test to establish the germinal force of a seed for oneself. After strewing out 100 seeds on a leaf of thin blotting paper, we wet the seeds and leave them in a warm, airy place for two days. As soon as the blotting paper dries up we wet it again. Even after two days it is easy to see which seeds are sprouting and which are not and when, after three days, we count the sprouting seeds we can determine the percentage of the valuable germinative and that of the dead seeds. When making such a test with a number of various compounds we are bound to discover differences of quality which, as a rule, accounts for the differences of price.

A number of fanciers contend that the quality of the seed we feed to our Budgerigars is of no great importance. Although I know such fanciers often obtain satisfactory breeding results, I want to brand such contentions as altogether erroneous. The war gave us opportunity enough to establish that while man, as a rule, will easily survive sharp rationing, a number of excessive feeders will actually thrive on it. Sufferers over many years from stomach, liver and kidney trouble suddenly felt new life! In the war, Budgerigar Mixture was hard to get and almost beyond the average man's means. People were forced to experiment with substitute seeds, and in that way a considerable number of Budgerigars actually survived the war. But it cannot be denied that the quality of the birds suffered badly, and there is very little doubt that the food was to blame for it.

Be that as it may, Budgerigars certainly need various types of canary seed as well as several kinds of millet seed. The canary seed (*phallaris canariensis*) is produced in southern Europe, Australia, Africa and Asia and will even grow here.

Naturally, the seed available at any bird or seed seller's is not always equal in quality. If we sow a little canary seed ourselves and hang up a bunch of ears with ripe or almost ripe seeds in the aviary or the cage, we do our pets a good turn that they will appreciate. As soon as we hang it up, the birds will make for and dispose of it in no time. This is a wonderful body-building food, particularly for young birds still in the nesting boxes.

Besides the canary seed, the birds need millet. This is produced in the same countries, and this, too, will grow here, although only for private use, for the quality of the home-grown millet will never be satisfactory enough to justify putting it on the market. The white brands are by far the best. The yellows range after these and the browns close the list. The well-known Senegal millet which is often sold as spray millet (in bunches), a delicacy for all tropical birds, is a wonderful food for Budgerigars.

There is, however, much difference of quality in seeds of the same brand. Several factors contribute to this difference. There is, for instance, the season of growth, the circumstances in which it was reaped and, finally, whether it was well dried and well cleaned. Seed is like wine: the year is as important as the house processing the harvest. That is why the layman should make it a rule to *buy seed only from a reputable firm*.

If it is decided to mix the food oneself, take one-third canary seed, one third white millet and one-third yellow millet. This mixture is based upon the assumption that the fancier will have to economize in the price, but if this is not the case, two-thirds canary seed and one-third white millet would do as well, if not better.

I do not, however, recommend using this compound all the year round. Like nearly all other animals, Budgerigars need an occasional change. This may be effected simply by changing the proportions of the compound now and then, but it is better to add some groats or clipped oats, especially in the spring.

It is obvious that the needs of birds will vary according to their age. Young birds need food with body-building elements. Moulting birds need food which, besides keeping their bodies thoroughly warm, will also provide foodstuffs for the growth of their new plumage. Birds raising young prefer green stuffs and ripening seeds. Birds being prepared for breeding need more minerals. During the winter, of course, warming food is essential.

It is not very difficult to satisfy these natural demands, and if we pay attention to them the results will never be disappointing. Clipped oats or groats favourably affect the mating impulse and thus are suitably added to the diet before the breeding period.

All so-called conditioners are a valuable addition to the diet when the birds are raising young. There are a number of very good brands available at the bird seller's. In the breeding period, a number of fanciers obtained excellent results by feeding the birds old whole-wheat or white bread, either soaked in milk or in water, in addition to the staple diet. If it is decided to adopt this practice, care should be taken to see that the bread is at least a few days old. This bread is soaked and then thoroughly pressed out. Only then should milk or water be added. Milk has, of course, the disadvantage of turning the bread sour in summer. This is dangerous, and if the bread has milk added to it, the remains should be removed every night.

Green foods are of *primary importance*, particularly in stocking up the birds' supply of vitamins. Such foods should not be omitted in any period or season. Chickweed, chicory, spinach and endive are nearly always available, and seeding grasses should be given in quantity all the summer.

A plentiful supply of oyster grit and mineral grit is very important, and crushed, dried, domestic hens' egg shells will also be valuable. Quite apart from the fact that the birds need the grit to help them grind the seeds in their stomachs, it also contains a number of minerals indispensable for bodybuilding purposes. Pieces of old mortar rubble will also be beneficial. And, last but not least, cuttle-fish bone should always be available.

Although it may seem from this that keeping Budgerigars is not as simple a business as one might have thought, I am sure that most people will not find it so difficult in the long run. Quite a number of indispensable foodstuffs may be given together for considerable periods and the rest will become a mere matter of habit and routine.

A final word about the high value of germinating seeds. There is an easy way to prepare these at home. After shaking some seed into a simple jam-jar, fill it up with water and leave it for the night. Next day renew the water and empty the contents of the jar into another jar which should be closed with a lid pierced with a number of small holes. The jar should then be turned upside down and allowed to drain slowly. On the following day the seeds, now visibly sprouting, may be fed to the birds. It is advisable not to prepare too much of this seed at once, as it will soon turn sour. The supply should never exceed the ration for a few days. To assist in its digestion a little fine charcoal (obtainable in special packings at almost every bird seller's) should be added.

In the following table a short list is given of the percentage content of seeds fed to Budgerigars.

	Crude Albuminoids	*Crude fats*	*Fluids*	*Ashes*	*Crude cellulose*	*Other carbohydrates*
Canary seed (*Phallaris canariensis*)	14·4	6·4	11·8	5	7·1	55·3
Millet (*Panicum and Setaria*)	11·3	4·2	11·7	3·8	8·5	60·5
Oats	11·3	5·6	11·2	3·4	11·6	56·9

I feel that this chapter should not be closed without a final warning. Budgerigars cannot live for long without food. Although practically everything else may be allowed to wait for a day or so, the seed-hopper or seed-vessel *must* be well supplied at all times. I have already mentioned the importance of drinking water. This should be renewed every day. Water for bathing, however, is not necessary.

6. DISEASES

Every fancier may be called upon to deal with the ailments to which his birds are liable. Although his management may be excellent and the food he gives his birds of the best quality, one or more birds may fall ill or even die. He should not leave it to chance to decide whether the birds recover or not, and if a dead bird has to be disposed of his responsibilities do not end there. It may be sent to a number of institutes engaging in research. In the interests of the hobby, he should try to find out with what kind of ailment or disease the birds suffered and what steps might have been taken to cure them.

Psittacosis

Birds dying from unknown causes obviously give more reason for alarm than birds dying from old age. There may be many reasons why they die, but the disease most to be dreaded is psittacosis, or parrot disease, which can also infect man. Owing to the use of Penicillin and Aureomycin, no recent cases of the disease which at first seems to be pneumonia proved fatal to the patient, so far as I am aware. Nevertheless, a number of disturbing articles on the subject published in the press many years ago are still causing alarm to many, and now and again the fear of psittacosis deters a bird fancier from keeping Parrots or Budgerigars. Still, it is undeniable that Parrots and Budgerigars are not the sole carries of the *virus* which causes the disease. It may be carried by other birds as well, e.g. canaries, poultry, ducks, pheasants, pigeons and wild birds. Those birds, however, seldom carry the virus and when they do the disease is far less serious. American scientific research workers have suggested that the disease should be called *ornithosis* as distinct from psittacosis, which is carried almost exclusively by Parrots and Budgerigars. Although birds carrying the virus may seem to be healthy, the disease may not become evident at once. It will become virulent only when the general condition of the birds deteriorates, just as persons in bad condition are more susceptible than healthy ones to any infection. Because so much has been said and written about the dangers of psittacosis, I should like to go into it more closely because, in my opinion, *the danger is now so small* that there really is no reason for anybody to shun or abandon the hobby on that account.

Former press agitation about the dangers of psittacosis once made the import of Budgerigars impossible. Lately bird lovers all over the world have protested against such reports, maintaining, with good reason, that the regulations controlling the import of the birds belong to time when modern remedies were not available to science and that an occasional death by psittacosis could not be prevented.

Investigation has proved the cause of the disease to lie invariably with the poor conditions under which mass imports have taken place, the birds being crowded into stuffy cages without light, fresh air and water. Under such conditions the health of the birds was liable to be impaired and the virus, always latent, was thus given full scope for dangerous development. The disease never appeared in a cage of birds that, for some years, had received proper attention in a living-room. In the United States, too, the authorities are still watchful, maintaining a strict ban on imports. In this country efforts were made to admit the birds after a period of strict quarantine. This procedure had its difficulties, as the virus, after remaining latent for as long as 8–10 months, may still develop when the condition of the birds takes a sudden turn for the worse.

Despite these restrictions many fanciers are trying to facilitate the admittance of the birds, and new bills recommending medical treatment of all birds to be imported in the United States have been submitted. Human beings who contract the disease may be cured by Aureomycin, and so can the birds. This is, no doubt, the specific treatment indicated by the new bills. In order to discover whether psittacosis is present a blood test must be made. As the symptoms resemble those of pneumonia, the family doctor is liable to make a wrong diagnosis. The disease does not follow a regular course, the fever receding and returning again and again. The layman, therefore, is apt to come to the conclusion that the apparent pneumonia might turn out to be parrot disease, after all. In view of the foregoing considerations I do not hesitate to advise the fancier to keep new birds bought from a reputable bird seller or from a well-known breeder in quarantine for at least six weeks. If the birds then turn out to be healthy, they may be admitted to the common aviary. They may of course prove to be ill, after all, but the chance is extremely slight.

Management of birds should be irreproachable in every respect. They must not be kept in a dark shed or a damp kitchen. If they are given airy, well-lighted accommodation, free from draught, they will not fall ill very easily.

In a case of death from unknown causes, a veterinary surgeon should be consulted or the dead bird should be sent to an institute for proper investigation. By doing this one protects, not merely oneself and one's own birds, but also other people's birds.

Cold

Having discussed the worst disease that may befall Budgerigars, it should be pointed out right away that to a layman neither this nor any other disease is easy to determine. The symptoms are always the same and easy to establish. When a sitting bird remains huddled up and its head hidden in its feathers, it is a sure sign that it is ill. Unfortunately, illness will invariably make the bird refuse to eat, and this alone is enough to cause death. If it is obvious that the bird caught a cold, it is advisable to put it in a sick-cage and keep it thoroughly warm. Instead of the staple diet, it is advisable to offer spray millet. Budgerigars relish spray millet which they may be tempted to eat. Recovery depends upon getting the bird to eat.

Intestinal trouble

Birds with intestinal trouble should be kept thoroughly warm. They should be given no green food and no cod-liver oil. Fine charcoal, a regular addition to the staple diet anyway, will usually yield favourable results.

French Moult

Now and then one hears of 'runners', chicks leaving the nest with insufficiently grown flight and tail feathers. A number of theories have been advanced about this disease, but up till now the scientists have failed to reach a unanimous verdict. Some are inclined to regard this peculiarity as a degenerative system; others attribute it to a certain mite; still others suggest that a lack of oxygen is at the root of it.

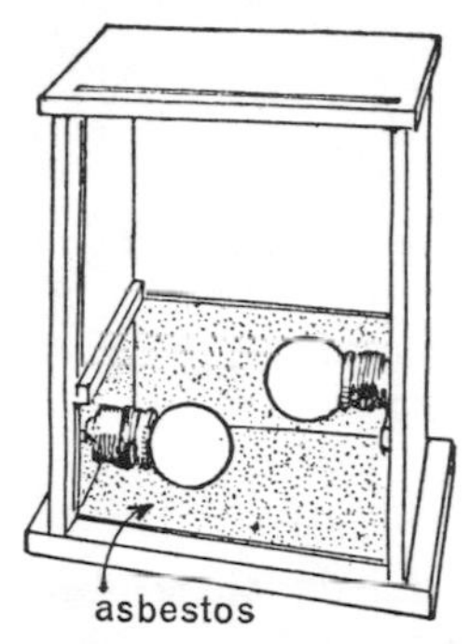

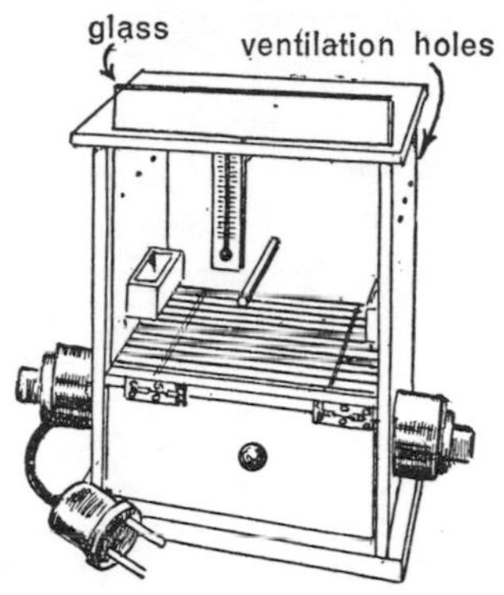

The hospital cage shown here on a very small scale may be built at home. The bulbs may be switched on separately, so as to regulate the temperature. A cage containing a thermostat, though offering considerable advantages, is usually too expensive for the purpose, though a thermometer is indispensable. A temperature of over 85° F *is allowable only in exceptional cases. It is obvious that the perch should not be fixed over one of the bulbs. A sick bird does not need much exercise and will usually stay quietly where it is. The window will allow us to watch the bird closely. The ventilation holes should be large*

There is something very remarkable about this French moult, but after the first moult, the birds will usually return to normal.

If a mite should be the cause of the trouble, spraying with the mixtures available for the purpose would be the correct solution. If a lack of oxygen should be to blame, this should not be difficult to remedy, either. But if it is a degenerative system the parents should not be bred from again. It seems to me that degeneration is probably the cause, as conclusive tests have shown that a bird having once produced 'runners' can always produce them again.

Dr. Steiner made a great number of tests with 'runners' and in his opinion proved the hereditary nature of the disease. Obviously, inbreeding may produce a strain of birds more susceptible to the disease than a strain regularly furnished with fresh blood. When debility sets in the former are liable to be more susceptible to the disease than the latter.

In my view, a good strain of birds, regularly provided with fresh blood and living under healthy conditions, accommodated in well-disinfected aviaries and nesting boxes, and getting the right vitamins in sufficient quantities with its food, is very unlikely to produce 'runners'.

Degeneration

While discussing degenerative systems I want to point out straight away that all birds born with abnormalities, i.e. with bow-legs, undershot beaks, etc., should be destroyed and even the parents should be dispensed with and should not be bred from again.

Moult

Moult is not really a disease but I deal with it in this chapter because the outward appearance of the birds at the time of moulting often leads people to think that the birds are in bad health.

The moult, usually setting in after the breeding period, may take various courses. Sometimes it will be over and done with in a few weeks. At other times it will be very slow, and might take months. The owners of moulting birds should take special care of them.

Unusual changes in temperature may cause moult. Birds returning from a show where, usually, the temperature is higher than in the open-air flight will often begin to moult immediately.

The best months for sending Budgerigars to an exhibition are September to December. By then the moult is usually finished and the birds are at their best. In the breeding period which starts as early as March, the hen's tail will curl up as a rule owing to the hatching she does in the nesting box.

Egg-binding

Egg-binding is not an unusual complaint among Budgerigars. But if it appears, bad management is always to blame. If Budgerigars get enough mineral grit and cuttle-fish bone they should not suffer from this complaint. If during the winter and despite the cold Budgerigars keep breeding, an occasional case of egg-binding may occur, but as soon as an affected bird is put into a warm cage, the egg will usually appear pretty quickly. A very young hen may also have difficulties with her first egg. In such a case the breeding organs have not developed sufficiently, and the hen should be left alone for another few months.

Vertigo

Vertigo may occasionally occur as a result of egg-binding. It is a form of neurosis which disables the hen, so that it cannot control its flight.

It will collide with everything, and even when sitting on the ground may be unable to maintain its equilibrium. Cod-liver oil and lime mixed with the food should prevent this disease. A hen suffering from vertigo should be put into a warm cage with a roof too low to enable her to fly. By taking cod-liver oil with the seed the bird may often be cured in a few days, but if after a week of such treatment there are no signs of a change for the better, the neurosis may be regarded as incurable.

Caked feet

Caked feet should first be soaked in warm water and Dettol and then dried with cotton wool.

Scaly Face

The condition known in the Budgerigar Fancy as Scaly Face not only attacks the cere but also the beak, the skin around the eyes, the legs and in extreme cases the wing butts. It usually first appears as small rough whitish lumps at the base of the cere and side of beak from where it will spread especially to the beak itself and perhaps the eye skins. Fortunately, although it is highly infectious, it can be easily and completely cured by applying as directed one of the patent creams or ointments sold at Bird Accessory Stores for this purpose. However, before any treatment is started the perches, wire mesh netting, seed and water vessels, should be thoroughly washed with a solution of Dettol and warm water. Several applications of the cream or ointment may be necessary before the condition has completely been cured. It may be a number of weeks before all traces of Scaly Face have completely disappeared.

7. REPRODUCTION

Many Budgerigar owners, besides colour breeders or Budgerigar fanciers, will want chicks from their birds. The adaptation of cages and aviaries to the purpose has been thoroughly dealt with and should be perfectly clear by now. So let us suppose everything is spick and span for breeding to start. The first step is to allot a cock to each hen, but before this is done due consideration must be given to the choice of the pairs in the hope that they will be mutually agreeable.

Usually the female will agree to the male selected for her, particularly if the precaution is taken of giving each pair a separate cage. Occasionally, however, a pair will refuse to have anything to do with each other. To deal with such contingencies, one has to hold a few substitute birds in reserve. The best method is to keep the cocks and the hens rigidly apart during the winter pause.

At the end of February or the beginning of March we put the pairs together, provide each of them with two nesting boxes and await events. The hen will probably soon begin to inspect the nesting boxes, and as a rule the cock will follow her closely, for nine out of ten Budgerigar cocks will insist upon carrying out their own private inspection of the inside as well as of the outside of the box. Now if there are enough perches to provide ample opportunity for a mating, we shall soon observe that, after the mating, the hen will make a bee-line for the nesting box to be fed, henceforth, by the cock. In fact, it is not at all unusual for the cock to start feeding the hen a day or so before the mating.

The first egg may be expected to appear after a few days although sometimes it will take a few weeks. By now, the fancier is watching the box day by day so that he may take a note of the day when the first egg appears. The others will then follow on alternate days until there are six or even eight of them. Usually the hen will stay in the nest as soon as the first egg is laid. The cock will feed her, and she will not leave the nest for more than a few minutes a day.

If there are several boxes of breeding Budgerigars and if, in one of them, there is a clutch of only four eggs whereas elsewhere there is a clutch of eight, we should take two from the latter and add them to the former although, of course, the eggs have to be marked carefully in doing this so that we may know to which parents the chick belongs. In this connection a correctly kept breeding register is an indispensable aid. Such a register will tell us how long the eggs in a given box will take to hatch, and it is obvious we may only balance clutches in this way if hatching periods of the nests agree.

The breeding calendar a Dutch seed house once sent to its clients is a very handy help in this respect. It showed columns for the number of the cage, the number of the cock and the number of the hen. It also showed the day the hen began to sit, the day the eggs were hatched, the number of eggs and finally the number of sound and addled eggs. A simple note book will suffice, and the pages can be ruled off in the following way:

Cock Colour and Number	*Hen Colour and Number*	*1st egg laid*	*Number of eggs*	*Number of chicks*	*Ring numbers young cocks*	*Ring numbers young hens*
osb/alb '84/5	oma '83/18	6·3·'85	5	4	'85 1·4	'85 2·5

This can then be read as follows:

'Cock Opaline Sky blue, split Albino, bred 1984 No. 5 × Hen Opaline Mauve; bred 1983 No. 18. First egg laid March 6 1985, 5 eggs, hatched 5, namely 2 cocks and 2 hens numbered 1 and 4, 2 and 5, the bird with Ring No. 3 having died.'

Such tabulated records will allow us to trace the pedigrees of every bird bred in our aviaries. If desired another column may be added giving the expectation, i.e. the colour of the chicks the pair should produce. In the above example this would be: sky blue × mauve gives 100% cobalt. Opaline × opaline gives 100% opaline. It follows all the Cobalts will be opaline! But as the cock was split albino, half of the young hens may be albino. Outwardly, the young cocks will all be alike, but half of them will be split albino again. As the appearance of the birds will not give any indication of this property, experiment will be the only means of establishing which cocks are split albinos and which are not. We still have to bear in mind the fact that the calculation of the percentage started from 100 chicks. Hence it is altogether possible for the first clutch merely to produce chicks that, outwardly, are all perfectly alike whereas two or three hens of the second clutch will be albinos. Now the albino factor is sex-linked, that is to say among the chicks issuing from an albino cock, only the hens will be visible albinos. Hens cannot be 'split' because they do not possess the sex chromosome to which the albino factor is linked.

If we find albinos or lutinos in a clutch neither of the parents of which is an albino or lutino, these young albinos or lutinos must be hens!

This is a sample of the sort of thing with which the second part of this book will deal.

The keeping of such a breeding register does not take much time, and it is indispensable to those wanting to breed carefully while going in for real 'colour production'. For anyone intending, for instance, to breed pure in order to build up a sound strain, the best starting point is a correctly kept register. By this time, it will also be obvious that, if we want to tell the chicks apart, separate breeding compartments are the sole possibility. Nor is the above mentioned trick of balancing clutches, by adding an occasional egg to another clutch, to be recommended if we do not carefully mark the egg or if we do not know exactly when it will hatch. If these conditions are missing, confusion will ensue, and the results will tell us nothing.

There is, however, an exception to this rule. If one knows that the issue of a given pair is certain to consist of, say, Blues and Lutinos, one may always add an egg certain to produce, say, either a Green or a Yellow. In that case, the colour will tell us which chicks belong to the agents and which are the foster children.

A description of various types of nesting boxes is given elsewhere.

One must always bear in mind that Budgerigar cocks are no paragons of virtue or matrimonial faith. Some fanciers will try and accustom the pairs to each other before allowing two pairs to breed in the same cage. In spite of this one may never be sure the chicks will belong to the chosen parents. More often than not one of the cocks will dominate the other and break up the mating.

A colour breeder will never put two breeding pairs into a single cage.

Nevertheless, some fanciers prefer to have a number of birds breeding together in a big aviary, and if all of them are pure breeders, for instance Lutinos or Greens or Blues or Yellows, there is no real

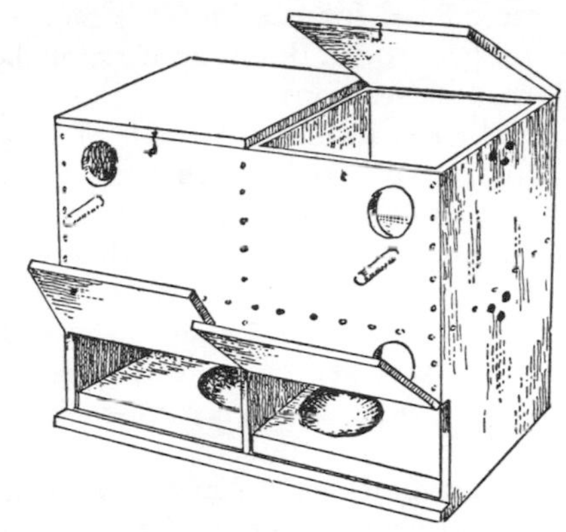

Double nesting box as used on the Continent

objection to this, as the chicks will be Lutinos, Greens, Blues or Yellows! In such a case, however, keeping a breeding register is out of the question.

If one insists on having all colours breeding together, the results can be extremely gay and colourful, but there is a distinct drawback to this method, as the hereditary factors of the chicks will then be inextricably mixed. Quite apart from this, experience proves that the colours of such chicks will gradually lose all depth and bloom and the dominant colour(s) predominate. The only way to obtain valuable and lasting results is by methodical breeding and careful selection.

Anyone intending to breed methodically has to choose between two possible alternatives. He may either buy birds of known pedigree, and this means buying them from an experienced colour breeder; or he may start with one or several pairs of birds bought at a show or a dealers, after he has consulted the colour tables in the second part of this book so as to establish the best combinations he should choose in order to breed a pure-bred stud of birds himself within a very short time. The latter alternative will certainly take somewhat longer but nobody can deny that there is added attraction in the thought of building one's own strain from the very beginning. In doing so, however, one should pay careful attention to every important detail such as type, number of spots of the necklace, shape of the head, carriage of the wings and, of course, the colour. Nowadays so many more or less indefinable birds are offered for sale that it is difficult to make one's choice without a proper model. But it can certainly be done, with the help of the coloured illustrations in this book.

A Budgerigar, as a rule, will not show its age; yet age is of great importance. Usually birds bred by colour breeders will carry a ring giving the year of birth. When buying at a dealers, it is best to purchase young birds, i.e. birds not yet showing a yellow-white ring around the eyes. The eyes of young birds are black. Very old birds may be recognized by the ceres that will turn dark and flaky with age. Remarkably enough, old cocks will get brown ceres like the hens instead of the original bright blue ones. If this is the case, it is a sure sign that the sexual organs have ceased to function.

It is not at all unusual for the first clutch to contain clear eggs. If this occurs it is possible that mating took place too late. In such circumstances, there may be only two chicks in this nest whereas a neighbouring nest may count six or seven of about the same age. Here it is completely right for the fancier to balance such nests by conveying some chicks from the crowded nest to the poor one although, of course, this should not be done until the rings are fitted, or we may be unable to keep the chicks apart. In order to facilitate this, it is desirable to take rings of different colours for different pairs of Budgerigars. The chicks of each pair then get rings of the same colour. The metal ring carrying the code, year and serial numbers may be fitted to the other foot. It is best to fit the rings when the chicks are five days old. The ring is first placed over the two front toes and then passed over the ball of the foot, after which it is slipped over the outward, rear toes, and does not hurt the bird in the least.

If nesting boxes are examined regularly and if, in so doing, one records the day of the first egg in the breeding book, this will enable one to calculate when there will be chicks in the next and when the rings will have to be fitted. It is very convenient to have a card fixed to each cage with these dates marked on it.

Hens may sometimes become very pugnacious. This may complicate things when more than one hen or more than one pair are occupying the same cage. In such a case, a hen may try and force her way into a box where another hen is quietly breeding. The cocks are not in the least concerned with female quarrels, which normally end in a fight and often lead to broken toes. As often as not the breeding hen is dragged from the box by the aggressor who then takes possession. It is obvious many an egg will get broken during such quarrels, and if the aggressor succeeds in taking possession of the nest, she will throw out all the eggs.

The only remedy is to remove the pugnacious hen to another cage, with or without her mate. This is another reason why the fancier should pay a quiet visit to the breeding cages now and then. He should never fail to keep a watchful eye on the boxes and their contents.

There is considerable difference of opinion as to the best age for a Budgerigar to begin to breed. Even though a fancier may induce early-born chicks to breed at the close of the same season, this certainly is not advisable. I had to try this once myself when I was endeavouring to take stock of a certain hereditary process and had no time to wait another year. I must admit the results were poor. The two clutches contained no more than three and four eggs, respectively, and only two and three chicks grew up, so I failed to get the results I was needing so badly. In fact, I did not get normal results until the second brood arrived and after the birds were more than eight months old. Birds born in April or May may not be used for breeding purposes until the following February or March and, if possible, the hen should be a few months older than the cock. Birds born as late as August or September should not be allowed to breed until the following June, and even then they should not rear more than one clutch. Although the birds are fully grown after six months it is unnatural for them to breed at that age.

When a hen has laid her first egg she will usually begin to sit straight away although, occasionally, she will wait for the second. On account of this, some eggs will take 20 days to hatch while others will merely take 18, the latter being the incubation period counting from the day when the hen begins to sit. During the whole of that period, the sitting hen is fed by the cock. When the eggs are first hatched, the hen alone feeds the chicks. The cock takes a hand again when the chicks are starting to feather. When, after 28 to 30 days, the chicks fly out both the hen and the cock will continue to feed them for some time. By a process similar to that taking place in the crop of a hen-pigeon hatching her eggs, a kind of crop milk is produced in the crop of the Budgerigar hen during the first days. This crop milk is the first food for the chicks. Afterwards the food she is given by the cock is mixed, in the crop, with various juices so as to render it fit for the chicks' digestive organs.

Dr. G. W. Buttner made a special study of this process, which is of first importance in the diet of Budgerigars. According to Dr. Buttner, the Budgerigars' milk, i.e. the crop milk with the seed, may not reach the correct consistency if the parents are not given the right food, and the chicks may then develop badly.

Not every hen appreciates a clean home. Some keep the box and the nestlings wonderfully clean but the majority are content to allow the household to wallow in filth, and if that happens we must intervene and clean out the box.

It is not unusual for a chick to die and the hen to leave it where it is, so that the other chicks just sit around on it. Now, if such a tiny body dries up not much harm is done, but if the chick happens to have grown a bit before dying the nest may become an awful mess. That is why we should continue to inspect the boxes after the eggs are hatched. When necessary we should clean the boxes as well as the feet of the chicks and keep an eye open for abnormalities, deformations, etc. The toes especially must be cleaned carefully as any negligence may cause the dirt to harden and to become very difficult to remove. It follows that, if the job is deferred until the chicks have flown out, there is a risk that a toe or a nail may be injured—and the nail, at least, will never grow again.

Occasionally complaints are made about chicks not hatching well and drying up some days before the eggs are due to hatch. Such trouble is caused by an extreme lack of humidity in the atmosphere. The only places where such mishaps occur are stuffy living-rooms or aviaries with all the nesting boxes fixed in the full heat of the sun or against a wooden wall, the rear side of which is in the full glare of the sun all day. In order to keep the eggs from drying up, we have to refix the boxes in a place giving more shade, or near an open window of the living-room so that moist air from outside may enter into it. That is why it is always best to arrange for Budgerigars to breed in the open air, i.e. in boxes fixed in the sheltered part of the open-air flight. When faced with trouble of this kind, a change of conditions is always the obvious solution. If this is impracticable, the eggs should be dipped into or sprayed with tepid water.

If the lack of humidity is not to blame, the cause is probably a lack of vitality in the chicks themselves, and the parents should be dispensed with. I myself have never had any dried-up eggs from my Budgerigars, but I have had some from other tropical birds, though only in the bird room. Budgerigars flying about in an open-air flight most of the time and having their nesting boxes as much in the open as possible will not produce badly hatched eggs. We have, however, to guard against lice and red mite. The birds as well as the nesting boxes must be freed from these pests, and with the help of the disinfectants available for the purpose the task should be an easy one.

Some fanciers prefer to remove the first two eggs, and refrain from restoring them until the third egg is laid. By acting in this way they are seeking to reduce the difference in the age of the chicks. As far as I can see there is not the slightest reason for this so long as the clutch does not exceed six eggs, and clutches exceeding this number should not be allowed to hatch anyway. In a clutch of six, the difference in the age of the chicks will usually not exceed ten days. This will cause no difficulty whatever; in fact it is the usual state of things in nature although, as a matter of fact, the average clutch in the wild will not exceed 4-5 eggs. If six chicks are too much for our purpose we may always transfer one chick to another box containing only three or four. In the breeding season, there usually is no scarcity of boxes with such small clutches.

Budgerigars are admirable foster-parents. They will rarely refuse to adopt a chick from another nest. Of course, the foster chick should be ringed so that we may always distinguish it from the rest. I repeatedly transferred an entire clutch of chicks, occasionally as much as ten days old, to another box even though, up till then, the new box contained only eggs which would not take long to hatch. The breeding hen was immediately prepared to rear the chicks when, in her own box, she found them instead of the eggs. The operation would never have succeeded if I had transferred the eggs with the box. As a matter of fact, I once fixed a box with half-hatched eggs in the place of another box also containing four eggs hoping that this hen which, as I remember, had just begun to sit, would hatch out the half-hatched eggs. At first she refused to enter the box, but after a few days, she decided to accept it, but threw out the half-hatched eggs and laid her own clutch. If I had just transferred the eggs to the box she was already using all might have been well.

Occasionally a hen rearing a clutch of chicks will start laying a second clutch while the chicks are still in the box. This is very disagreeable, as the eggs will get very dirty as a rule. The way to deal with this is to transfer the chicks to another box placed immediately beside the first. It is almost certain the cock will then rear the first clutch thus allowing the hen to devote her attention to the second clutch. She will start by cleaning the box thoroughly and henceforth will not give the first clutch another thought.

The same method will hold good where the hen begins to pluck or bite off the feathers as soon as the chicks begin to fledge. This may lead to lasting damage because, more often than not, the plumage will never become normal again, not even after the moult. As feather-plucking appears to be a hereditary inclination I definitely advise the exclusion of such hens and their young from further breeding.

This also applies to birds showing other bad qualities that, being hereditary, we do not want reproduced in our strain, such, for example as birds killing their own chicks or birds that show malformations not caused by injury. Even chicks showing certain deficiencies in type should not be kept if we want to breed beautiful birds. As a matter of fact, we should keep only chicks that, in type as in colour, are at least equal to, and possibly better than, the parents. All birds differ from one another, not only in colour and markings, but also in size, carriage of the wings, position of the eyes and the shape of the skull. Readers should compare them with picture of the ideal Budgerigar (Page 16). There is actually a superabundance of inferior birds, products of injudicious breeding, which are produced at an attractive price to meet a steady demand. Nevertheless, there will always be a demand for really good birds.

Although Budgerigars will go on breeding all the year round, it is advisable to limit these activities to the best period, i.e. between the beginning of March and the end of September. During the winter months when moulting occurs, we should leave them a period of rest. We should keep the cocks and the hens apart and give them plenty of opportunity to fly about and gain new strength. Older Budgerigars may be kept in the open-air flight all winter if we provide adequate shelter for the night. In this shelter put the drinking water and the seed hopper. The birds will then automatically stay in for their night's sleep. During the day Budgerigars will stay outside as a rule, no matter how cold the weather may be.

I strongly advise breeding not more than two clutches in a single season. Three or even four clutches in a row are too much of a strain on the hen. After the second clutch, the breeding period should be closed by removing the nesting boxes.

Many fanciers are apt to forget that the breeding season is a severe strain on the cock, too. It is the cock which feeds the hen as long as she is breeding and, more often than not, takes care of the chicks as well. Occasionally, cocks will die from sheer exhaustion. For this reason, a clutch should be limited six eggs. It is obvious that a nest of four or five will thrive better than one of six or even eight. Well-nourished chicks will turn into stronger and better developed birds.

A few weeks after leaving the boxes and beginning to fly the chicks should be transferred to a special training aviary designed to give them adequate opportunity for development. A bird as vivacious as a Budgerigar needs plenty of flying space. It is the only means for the bird to develop fully its vigour and beauty. In such a training aviary with chicks, nesting boxes are, of course, prohibited.

At the close of the season birds should be classified. We carefully select the specimens destined to help building our strain. If we want to enter some of them at a show we separate them from the others and put them in a roomy cage. Birds which have spent their youth in an aviary will take some time getting used to a cage. Further advice on this point is given in Chapter 9.

8. APPLIANCES FOR CAGES AND AVIARIES

It is hardly necessary to point out we must find appropriate receptacles for the food we provide for our Budgerigars. We may use a deep flower-pot tray for the purpose but if we do the birds are likely to scatter the seed all over the cage.

So-called seed-hoppers are available in many different types, one of which is pictured on page 135. Some lack a drawer for the husks, and these are not recommended because the Budgerigars will make a terrible mess.

There are others showing a closed front, i.e. a front without a glass-plate. These are definitely dangerous because they do not show at a glance whether the birds have food enough. As Budgerigars cannot go without food for long, such hoppers may prove fatal. The hopper must be furnished with a glass plate and a drawer for the husks.

For the cuttle-fish bone we may buy or construct a clamping screw or a small rack.

The salt brick may be left lying around on the floor of the cage. The floor sand is strewn with oyster grit. When using the special floor sand available at the Bird Accessory Store, the addition of grit is unnecessary as the sand contains all the necessary minerals. An earthenware tray containing the necessary mineral grit may be put in a corner of the aviary.

For green food, too, a little rack is preferable since, as mentioned, Budgerigars are always apt to make a mess.

The drinking vessel may be hung from the top or placed in the middle of the cage. The best vessels are the upturned receivers in a porcelain tray or the normal upturned flasks in a zinc hanger. It is best to fix such zinc hangers to the wall of the cage providing a perch in front of it.

I want to close this chapter by discussing several types of nesting boxes and blocks appropriate for the purpose.

I have already expressed the opinion that there is no objection to

Type of seed-hopper

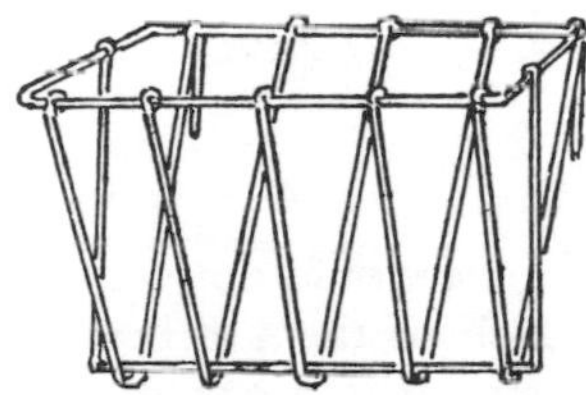

Rack for green food or cuttle-fish bone

the usual birch or poplar nesting box provided it is roomy enough. It is very decorative and if fixed with an eye to practical requirements there is no harm done if, for the purpose of nest control, we take it off for a moment and put it back again. However, if the lid turns on a screw and the screw is fixed accurately on one side it is not even necessary to take the box off: the opening of the lid will enable us to peep inside.

The fancier may choose between square boxes or oblong ones fashioned out of hardboard or wood. There are so many different types that it would take too long to mention them all.

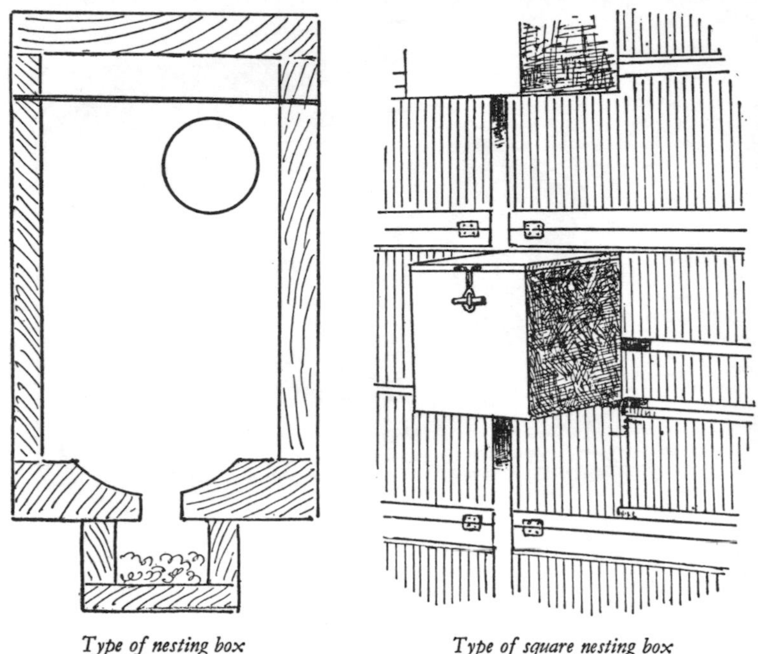

Type of nesting box with egg trap

Type of square nesting box

Pictures are given of some of them, but we would not venture an opinion as to their quality or decide which of them is best. Budgerigars are apt to breed in almost any box. My advice is to build or buy them with a view to easy cleaning and easy nest control without disturbance to the birds.

I have already pointed out that it is possible to have an entire colony breeding together. The result is a kind of inhabited flat. It is not at all unusual for box upon box to be sheltering a separate family.

A special box has even been invented for hens likely to break their eggs. It was illustrated in *Cage Birds* 1953. In the pit of the hollow, such a box is furnished with a hole somewhat larger than an egg. As soon as the hen lays her egg in the hollow the egg will pass through the hole. Under the hole is a small trap box with a little cotton wool.

The egg is unbroken and may then be put under another bird. It is clear that we should only go to such trouble with a very special hen we do not want to dispense with because the qualities she possesses are needed for our strain. I mention this just to show what powers of invention fanciers possess. The real fancier will find a solution for almost any difficulty he may meet with.

If we furnish a wall with a series of breeding cages, for example, three tiers of five in a row, each of them 20–24 in. (51–61 cm) high and 20 in. (51 cm) deep, their length varying from 30–36 in. (76–91 cm), it is advisable to provide a platform or cupboard under the cages to store seeds and materials. In such a case it is also preferable to fix the nesting boxes to the outside so as to avoid opening the cages to inspect the boxes for eggs. The seed-hoppers should then be built in the shape of a narrow drawer which may be opened daily so that we can blow off the husks and replenish the seed supply. The drinking vessels may be fixed inside the cage and as they are of glass we can always keep an eye on the water supply. Small basins fixed to the outside of the cage may serve quite as well if a perch is provided in front of them.

The breeding cages are furnished with drawers which can be sanded to facilitate cleaning. The measurements of the nest boxes may differ, but a space of at least 5 in. × 5 in. (13 cm sq.) is indispensable. The height of the boxes may be 8 in. (20 cm) or more and the entrance hole should be about $1\frac{1}{2}$ in. (4 cm) diameter. It should not be in the middle, but at the top and a little to the left or to the right. The hollow in the bottom should be on the opposite side. The bird entering the box will alight on the floor beside the hollow and walk up to the clutch. This is better than an entrance hole immediately over the eggs which may cause the hen to damage the eggs when she enters the box in a hurry. Below the entrance hole on the outside a perch should be fixed as the cock is liable to use it quite a lot during the breeding period, particularly when feeding the hen. There is no particular necessity for the perch, though, as Budgerigars often prefer to hang on to the nest from the outside.

As the hen likes to sit in the entrance hole, thus cutting off much of the air supply, it is important to provide round ventilation holes near the tops of all nesting boxes. The chicks may not die from lack of air, but it is clear we should provide for an adequate supply.

A practical move is to build boxes with a loose bottom provided

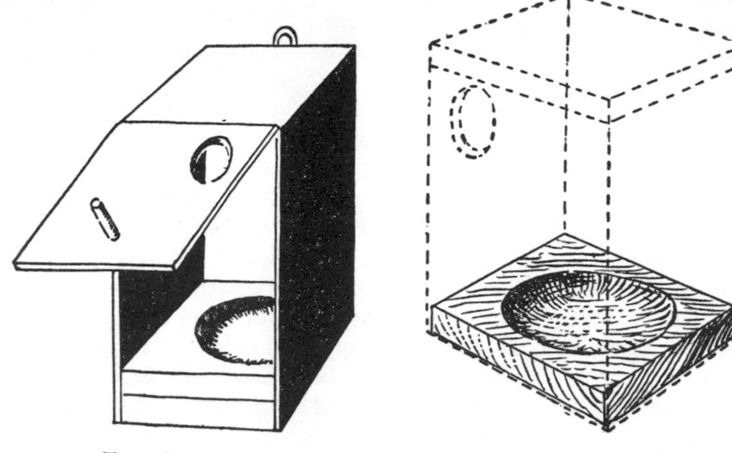

Type of nesting box

'Cardboard' nesting box with wooden concave bottom

with the necessary hollow. If the chicks make a terrible mess and the hen fails to clean it up, the soiled bottom may then be easily exchanged for a clean one.

A small quantity of soft pine sawdust put on the concave nest bottoms when the nest boxes are given to the pairs will help to keep the boxes sweet and dry. If the soiled sawdust is periodically removed and renewed, the chicks will always be in a clean, healthy condition.

9. BUDGERIGARS ON SHOW

Many a fancier will like to get an opinion on his birds now and then, and if he is a member of a local society, or of a national organization, he will have an opportunity to get his birds judged either at a local show or at a national exhibition.

For this purpose, every cage bird society will engage judges accustomed to judge the birds by common standards. For Budgerigars, special Budgerigar judges will be engaged, and judges with a wide experience and a well-established practice certainly deserve our confidence.

Anyone whose aim is to build up a special strain of Budgerigars of a given colour, and who is beginning to achieve his object, ought to know whether his birds can stand up to a critical inspection or whether the material he is using is adequate for his purposes. If the birds he is using are not good enough, he may still switch in good time to better birds. Exhibitions will provide the fancier with an opportunity to add a good bird or birds to his collection.

Quite apart from the facilities it provides for getting birds judged, membership of a national society will, as a rule, also provide the fancier with a brochure or magazine giving many useful hints for his fancy. Again the lectures and excursions organized by most societies are often of great importance. Lectures, visits to other breeders' birdrooms and bird parks are arranged by most societies and these prove of great value to their members.

Owing to the methodical work of the societies, there is now little uncertainty regarding the age and breeder of the birds put on exhibition and offered for sale.

In England, Budgerigar-keeping has become a national hobby. Between 2,000 and 3,000 birds are sent in every year to the National Exhibition, London and organized by 'Cage and Aviary Birds'. The membership of the Budgerigar Society exceeds several thousand, and entries at their annual Club Show are between 4,000 and 5,000. There is no doubt that, in addition to these, the Fancy numbers tens of thousands of enthusiastic adherents. As a result of this enthusiasm, the establishment of standards for the judging of Budgerigars in their various colours has made more progress in England than anywhere else in the world, and one of its features is a better scale of points. The main difficulty in setting up such a scale lies in the establishment of standards covering all standardized colours and colour varieties. With these standards established, we may then proceed to project a scale of points for the various kinds while keeping in mind the peculiarities of some varieties. These demand that certain qualities be rated very high for one kind, while they are entirely absent in another. The spots, for instance, disappeared with a number of varieties, and even the undulated pattern of the plumage responsible for the Budgerigar's scientific name will be found to be completely missing in several colour classes.

The British standard is undoubtedly the best available and is given below:

Scale of Points NOTE. CONDITION IS ESSENTIAL	*Size, Shape, Balance and Deportment*	*Size and Shape of Head*	*Colour*	*Mask and Spots*	*Wing Markings*
Green (Light, Dark or Olive)	45	20	15	15	5
Grey Green (Light, Medium or Dark)	45	20	15	15	5
Yellow (including Opaline Yellow but excluding Lutino	45	20	35	—	—
Olive Yellow (including Cinnamon Olive Yellow)	45	20	35	—	—
Sky Blue, Cobalt, Mauve or Violet	45	20	15	15	5
Grey (Light, Medium or Dark)	45	20	15	15	5
White (Light Suffusion) (including Opaline White but excluding Albino)	45	20	*35	—	—
Whitewing and White (Dark Suffusion)	45	20	*35	—	—
Yellow-wing (Light, Dark, Olive or Grey Green)	45	20	*35	—	—
Greywing (Light, Dark, Olive or Grey Green)	45	20	10	10	15
Greywing (Sky Blue, Cobalt, Mauve, Violet or Grey)	45	20	10	10	15
Cinnamon (Light, Dark, Olive or Grey Green)	45	20	15	15	5
Cinnamon (Sky Blue, Cobalt, Mauve, Violet or Grey)	45	20	15	15	5
Fallow (Light, Dark, Olive or Grey Green)	45	20	15	15	5
Fallow (Sky Blue, Cobalt, Mauve, Violet or Grey)	45	20	15	15	5
Lutino	45	20	35	—	—
Albino	45	20	35	—	—
Opaline (Light, Dark, Olive or Grey Green)	45	20	†15	15	5
Opaline (Sky Blue, Cobalt, Mauve, Violet or Grey)	45	20	†15	15	5
Opaline Cinnamon (Light, Dark, Olive or Grey Green)	45	20	†15	15	5
Opaline, Cinnamon (Sky Blue, Cobalt, Mauve, Violet or Grey)	45	20	†15	15	5
Opaline Greywing (Light, Dark, Olive or Grey Green)	45	20	†15	15	5
Opaline Greywing (Sky Blue, Cobalt, Mauve, Violet or Grey	45	20	†15	15	5
Yellow-faced (All varieties in Blue series except Pieds)	45	20	15	15	5
Pied (Recessive varieties)	45	20	‡15	—	20
Pied (Clear-flighted varieties)	45	20	15	15	§5
Pied (Dominant varieties)	45	20	‡15	15	‡5
Dark-eyed Cleat varieties	45	20	*35	—	—
Lacewings	45	20	15	15	5
Crested or Tufted varieties	45	20	†15	15	5
Spangles	45	20	15	15	5

* Points allocated for depth of colour and clearness of wings.
† Including clear mantle. ‡ Including contrast in variegation.
§ Including clear flights and tail.

Teams of six birds of any one colour *or* teams of four birds of any one colour.
Points: General quality 50. Uniformity 50.

Such a scale of points will, naturally, make higher demands on the judges, but it is liable to give more satisfaction, and it will enable breeders to continue quietly building up their special strain without running the risk that, on account of a primitive scale of points, their birds will be judged incorrectly and rated unnecessarily low.

The main task lies in the establishment, for every variety, of a standard description deviations from which ought to be prohibited. Birds not covered by this description should be excluded from adjudication, or they should be provisionally admitted to a general class. Obviously, this general class should then also include new varieties that, in the future, might come to be standardized varieties.

This scale of points will show that, in certain birds, colour is rated very highly whereas wing markings and spots are sometimes lacking altogether. Normal yellow birds will usually show a green, normal white birds a blue suffusion, and it is very difficult to breed Yellows or Whites showing no suffusion at all. That is why, in such cases, colour is rated so high.

In the first place it is, of course, of paramount importance to reach a definite agreement on the question of how a bird should look in order to fulfil the category indicated by its denomination, but it should not be difficult to provide a good specimen of each category, either alive or stuffed, for a special conference of judges to be held for the purpose. With this requirement in mind, I have included a number of coloured pictures of various birds. The illustrations invariably start out with the ideal model and the correct pose, even though this might occasionally imply that the birds were liable to look somewhat stiff, because only a limited number of attitudes were suitable for illustration.

The Budgerigar Society's Standard for the Ideal Budgerigar is as follows:

Condition is essential. If a bird is not in condition it should never be considered for any award.

Type—Gracefully tapered from nape of neck to tip of tail, with an approximately straight back line, and a rather deep nicely curved chest.

Length—The ideal length is 8½ in. from the crown of the head to the tip of the tail. Wings well braced, carried just above the cushion of the tail and not crossed. The ideal length of the wing is 3¾ in. from the butt to the tip of the longest primary flight, which must contain seven visual primary feathers fully grown and not broken. *No bird showing 'Long-flighted' characteristics shall be eligible to take any award.*

Head—Large, round, wide and symmetrical when viewed from any angle; curvature of skull commencing at cere, to lift outward and upward, continuing over the top and to base of head in one graceful sweep.

Beak—Set well into face.

Eye—to be bold and bright, and positioned well away from front, top and back skull.

Neck—to be short and wide when viewed from either side or front.

Wings—Approximately two-fifths the total length of the bird, well braced, carried just above the cushion of the tail and not crossed.

Tail—to be straight and tight with two long tail feathers.

Position. Steady on perch at an angle of 30 degrees from the vertical, looking fearless and natural.

Mask and spots—Mask to be clear, deep and wide, ornamented by six evenly spaced large round throat spots, the outer two being partially covered at the base of the cheek patches, the size of the spots to be in proportion to the rest of the make-up of the bird as shown in the Ideals published by The Budgerigar Society. Spots can be either too large or too small.

Legs and feet—Legs should be straight and strong, with two front and two rear toes and claws firmly gripping perch.

Markings—Wavy markings on cheek, head, neck, back and wings to stand out clearly.

Colour—Clear and level and of an even shade.

FAULTS IN BUDGERIGARS WHICH SHOULD BE PENALISED BY JUDGES

1. CONDITION IS ESSENTIAL—any bird out of condition should be penalised.
2. No bird showing long-flighted characteristics is eligible to take any award.

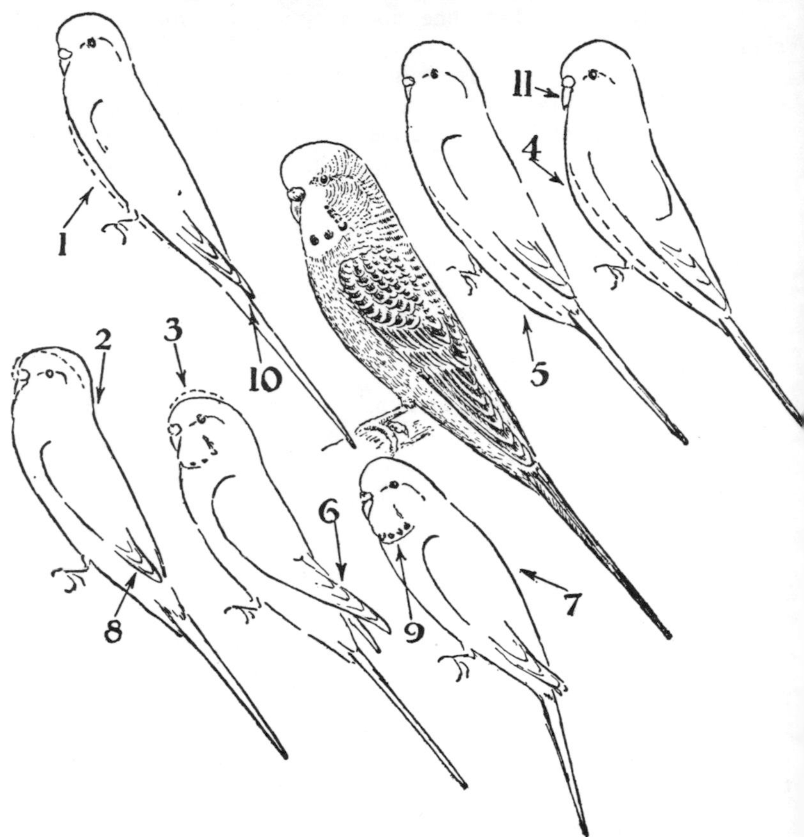

1. Too slim; 2. Pronounced nape of neck; 3. Dome too flat; 4. Pronounced chest; 5. Paunch; 6. Crossing flight ends; 7. Roach back; 8. Wings too short; 9. Too many spots; 10. Wings too long; 11. Protruding beak

3. Flecked headed birds should be penalised. A bird may win its class but cannot be considered for any special award.
4. Birds which have had flash spots removed.
5. Dominant Pieds showing completely clear wings.
6. Birds showing scaly-face around beak or legs should be removed from staging.

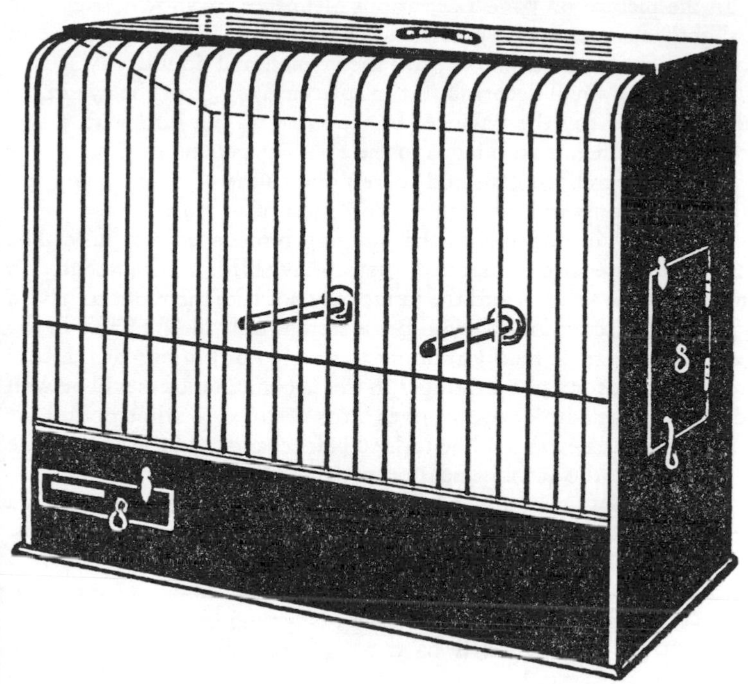

'B.S. Standard Show Cage' incorporating Patent No. 755106
By kind permission of The Budgerigar Society

7. Dominant Pieds having rings around the head.
8. Normals—Birds showing opaline characteristics on wings, neck and back.
9. Opalines and Cinnamon Opalines—Birds showing dark feathers in mantle and neck, foul tails, bad wing markings.
10. White-wings and Yellow-wings showing pale cheek patches, pale body colour or cinnamon wings.
11. Lutinos showing green suffusion or wing markings.
12. Albinos showing blue suffusion or wing markings.
13. Yellowfaces showing mask colour running into body.
14. Birds with mis-shaped spots.
15. Any bird not complying with the written standard.

In the picture on page 144 various blemishes are shown, usually in a slightly exaggerated degree to accentuate them. The appearance of the birds should be balanced, and the layman will doubtlessly see for himself that a small deformity or misplacement, e.g. of the eye in the head, will destroy the balance. In the same way, a bird with a low front or a paunch is an offence to the eye. The general carriage of the bird on the perch, too, should correspond to the drawing, being upright and strong and giving an impression of vigour.

Everyone will understand that judging birds is no easy task. The birds to be rated are not stuffed, they are live birds accommodated in small exhibition cages, and the judge may not take them out to have a good look at them in his hand. Birds tremulously hiding away in the back of the cage or madly running to and fro or tugging at the bars are unsuitable for a good rating. On this account, fanciers will be well advised to take a little trouble over birds destined to win trophies for their owners. They should be trained beforehand, and they need time to get used to the accommodation provided for them at the show.

There is no world standard for show cages, but there certainly is a British one, this cage being 14 in. long, 12 in. high and 6½ in. wide. (35 × 30 × 17 cm). A picture of it is given above.

Last, but not least, is the question of training the birds for exhibition. I have pointed out before that birds having lived in an open-air flight all the summer will have to get accustomed to the cage. Although this certainly does not mean that we have to put them into the exhibition cages at once, it is quite clear that any cage will mean a severe curtailment of the freedom they have grown up to enjoy. In order to accustom them to this, we should put each of them into one of the breeding cages that, at this time of the year, will be out of use. These cages must, however, be thoroughly cleaned for, as from now on, the birds themselves must be kept scrupulously clean. The bottom of the cage is covered with pure dry sand and cleaned regularly. If the shows start in November the birds selected for exhibition should be transferred to these cages at least a month before. As a rule, they will have their moult first.

The best way of washing a Budgerigar is to hold it in the hand and pass a lather brush with sufficiently warm soapy water very carefully over its feathers, taking good care always to rub in the direction of the feather. After this, we keep it wrapped in a bathing towel until it is well dried. We then put the bird back into the cage and fix a heating lamp or a small electric heater in front of it. At this time, draughts are of course more dangerous than usual. Never give the bird a complete bath; it will get much too wet.

A fancier accustomed to sending his birds to shows will probably find this practice less odd than beginners who, I know, are apt to consider such trouble unnecessary.

I strongly advise everyone to let the birds get used to the show cage for at least a week. By that time they will usually feel completely at home in it. They will display themselves gracefully, allowing the judge and the visitors to observe them thoroughly, this being one of the principal requirements of exhibition birds.

When discussing moult, I pointed out it is not at all unusual for birds returning from a show to begin to moult. Show halls are usually kept rather warm, and the change of temperature is apt to make them moult. A bird having moulted just before the show will not moult again. If, from an indoor aviary, birds are transferred to a show held during a period of severe cold, it is definitely inadvisable to transfer them to an open-air flight as soon as they return, as they may thus get pneumonia. Changes should always be gradual.

I should like to close this chapter on exhibitions with a tip for those fanciers who, perhaps months previous to the great day, discover their favourite to be flying about with a broken tail, a mishap from which, after all, any bird may suffer. When the tail feathers are extracted with care they will grow again in some six or eight weeks. If, on the other hand, one waits for the tail to be cast with the moult, it may take months, and the bird will be useless for the show.

10. TRAINING BUDGERIGARS AND TEACHING THEM TO TALK

Although this book is certainly not intended to further the training of circus performers and although, in my country, I only heard occasional rumours about talking and performing Budgerigars, there are too many examples of the phenomenon to leave it out of discussion altogether.

In the United States and France particularly, many Budgerigars were trained to give small private shows. On the backflap of the French treatise *La Perruche Ondulée* by R. Carpentier, one sees a charming young lady holding a long tress of hair in a graceful curve while allowing six trained Budgies to swing to and fro on it.

In the American Cage-Bird Magazine I often found photographs of Budgerigars riding around on the ladders of toy firemen's trucks or going up and down on a see-saw or even careering about in toy motor cars, and there is a wealth of anecdotes about Budgies making funny remarks or even reciting verse.

Nowadays talking Budgerigars are no exception in England, or in Germany either, and I am rather inclined to believe that many a fancier hearing only now what possibilities a Budgerigar has as a housemate will experience a desire to have such a playmate for himself. It requires time and patience to make such a small companion into a dear little friend whose favourite place is our shoulder, a faithful comrade always enjoyed in the company of its master or its mistress. Still, the result is worth all the trouble, particularly when a prolonged illness confines us to an armchair or even to our bed.

The well-known African Grey Parrot, the Yellow- or Blue-fronted Amazon and the Lesser Sulphur-crested Cockatoo are very eager to learn to imitate, and this agreeable quality certainly is one of the main reasons for the popularity of these creatures as cage birds. On the other side of the account are their disagreeable shrieking, a sometimes dangerous inclination to bite, and rather expensive feeding and accommodation requirements. Now if one knows that, after these birds, the Budgerigar is easily the best talker and imitator and if one considers how ridiculously cheap it is to buy, what modest requirements it has as regards food and accommodation, and what a model of devotion it can become, I think the talking Budgerigar has a great future in all countries.

In his famous work, Brehm mentioned all the capabilities of the Budgerigar of his day, and his record was followed by so many different reports that it will hardly be necessary to mention everything Budgerigars were taught to say. There is however a marked difference compared with the parrots. Among the vowels, Budgerigars prefer the *a* as in *lane* and the *e* as in *weed*, whereas the *a* as in *last* and the *o* as in *lone* are the basic vowels of the talking parrots. Children's and women's voices, however, are the organs which do these light vowels full justice, and that is why children and women are the best teachers for Budgerigars. Moreover, children and women are more likely than men to find time for teaching purposes, quite apart from the fact that, as a rule, they are more often at home than the men.

One of the outstanding qualities of Budgerigars is their love of company. On account of this, a Budgerigar living alone, i.e. without other birds of his kind, will soon begin to look around for other company. It follows that we should never try and keep two Budgerigars together while teaching them both to talk. They will be concerned exclusively with each other and keep talking their own Budgerigar language!

When separating a Budgerigar from his kind and giving him a place in the living-room, we should realize that, from then on, it will be our duty to give him regular attention to make up for the loss of his playmates.

If, in the course of my remarks, I have talked of 'him', I have done so on purpose as males are the most suitable for training as talkers.

The task is, of course, to find a suitable male. Among Budgerigars, as among human beings, not everyone is fit to go to high school! We need luck in making our choice and if—as a rule after a few months—we have made no progress, there is no alternative but to look for another candidate.

How shall we go about it? From a clutch of chicks between one week and three weeks old, in fact, a clutch just fledging, we select a young male. It is not very easy, though, to recognize a male at this age as then all ceres are a rather bluish rose. The bluest ceres and the highest domes may be considered to be indications of male chicks. At this stage chicks will hardly bite, so we had better leave the 'bite' test alone. The fact that hens will usually bite more firmly and hold on may help us to determine the sex of older chicks if we decide to wait a little longer. In doing so, we save ourselves considerable trouble for it certainly is no easy task to rear a three weeks' chick until it will eat by itself. As for taming it, there is no harm in waiting until they are a little older before we start on this, although we have to realize that taming will then take somewhat longer because the bird has got used to flying around with its kind. The talking lessons, however, must wait until the taming is done. To make sure, I shall discuss both methods.

Suppose we decide to adopt the first. We put the young fledgling into a cigar box, the bottom of which has been covered with a layer of sawdust. Instead of the lid, we use a piece of wire netting to close it. We put the box in some place in the living-room, taking care to select not too bright a spot. Being used to the semi-darkness of the log, the bird will tuck its head into a dark corner so that it will see as little light as possible. It will get used to the light after a time. It is hardly feasible to try and feed the chick in the dark just because it is used to it. On the other hand, all the trouble we are going to take in feeding the chick will not produce any result if we do not accustom the bird to the daylight at the same time!

When we take a chick out of the log, it is usually well-nourished and its crop is full, so we do not start feeding it straight away. We prefer to wait for about four hours in order that we may be sure that the bird is then hungry.

During the first week, we shall have to feed the chick six times a day, i.e. every three hours, just like a baby. And the curious part of it is we may give it the same food we give a baby. The nursing bottle is out of place, of course, but we may mix the infants' food into a pap and we may even use other farinaceous foods.

I myself prefer to use an ear or nose dropper to feed such chicks. In order to be able to do this, I make the pap, or the other soluble farinaceous food, just thin enough for the dropper to suck it in. Then I test the pap for the correct temperature (98° to 99° F), and feeding may start. The temperature of the pap is kept steady on a tea-warmer or by putting the vessel in hot water. The task of feeding the chick may not be an easy one at first. Putting a paper or a piece of cloth on our knee, we take the chick in our left hand and then put it down on the paper or the cloth in such a manner that the head peeps out of our hand. With the nails of the left and right index fingers we then open the little beak, push the dropper not too far into its throat and slowly press it out. If we do not push the dropper in too far we shall soon see that the bird starts to help with its tongue. After a few times it will open its beak all by itself, and by then there is no harm in allowing it to sit on the table and let it eat out of the dropper, which we press out as we go. We just have to make sure that the pap is kept at the correct temperature and take good care that the bird's crop is full after the operation. As soon as the bird wants to eat of its own accord, we may switch over to a teaspoon and mix hulled millet into the pap. When crushed a bit the millet will easily lose the husk. With a piece of cloth and warm water we carefully clean the little beak and the feathers around it after each meal. Otherwise the pap will dry up and get hard, thus becoming very difficult to remove.

As you see, there is a busy week or two ahead of us. But the results will be worth while. The bird will grow quite tame and welcome the food with loud chirps. It will run up to us, and very soon it will even come flying to meet us as, in the meantime, the feathers will have grown, causing it to start flying exercises. This means the time will have come to take it out of the box and transfer it to the cage we have set aside for it. As soon as it is in the cage it will try and reach the perch which we have purposely fixed near the bottom. Once it has taken possession of the perch, this will come to be its usual place. We now cover the bottom of the cage with millet. At first we still use crushed seeds, so that the chick may have no difficulty in removing the husks. Afterwards we switch over to ordinary millet and canary seed. We must still watch the little thing carefully. If it does not eat enough we should add some soaked farinaceous food.

Good care should be taken of our new room mate, putting at his disposal all the nourishment needed to help him grow up well. We mix some grit with the bottom sand, and mineral grit with the seed. Now and then we also add some drops of vitamins, and it will not be long now before we begin to give him some leaves of chickweed or chicory as a special treat.

The bird should not always be shut up in a cage. He must have his daily flying exercises in the room, and there is no need to frown at the thought of what will happen to the chairs and curtains, for the bird's small excreta are easily disposed of. They are practically dry and leave no stains as the bird drinks very little and eats nothing but farinaceous food.

By the time our Budgie comes and sits on our finger when we hold it out to him in his cage and allows us to carry him off without the slightest sign of fear, we may consider we have won his confidence. In the beginning he will occasionally be scared and fly off when we make an unexpected movement, but in the long run he will get used to this, too, and our shoulder will then become his favourite perch. Personally, I do not hold with the habit of clipping the wings a little on either side, so that he may only fly off with difficulty and never get farther than the table or the sideboard. There is always a danger that he may miscalculate the power of his wings, collide with something and hurt himself. With a little patience, we shall always get him to go wherever we want him, even if it may take a further week's training.

Now we can start with the lessons. To give these we must be alone with him, as every diversion draws his attention. When other persons (even children) are in the room it is useless to hope for the slightest attention. It is also advisable to give the lesson at regular hours so that this, too, may become a habit. The twilight hour, when the bird himself is inclined to become restful after a busy day, when he has had his meal and is prepared to give us his attention, is eminently suited to the purpose. He must be able to see his mistress clearly and when he sits on her finger he will listen to her pronouncing his name. This must have an *ee* sound in it if it is to suit the bird's talents. Peter, or Beebee, for instance, would do, but there are of course many other names for the choosing. When he hears his mistress's voice he will reply in his own chatter at the beginning, but after a day or so the trainer will notice that, almost by accident as it were, he will be making the sounds he picked up during the day, and sooner or later his name will be one of them. Daily exercise at a regular hour and a tireless repetition of the name will bring their results. Some birds will react quickly, and in such cases we may soon add other words or even a complete sentence. Some birds learn slowly or not at all. A few weeks will tell us what to think of our candidate. If he is unable to imitate any sounds, neither the creaking of the door nor the signal we whistle for him every day nor even his own name, he is a hopeless case and we had better look around for a more talented pupil. As a rule, however, we shall not be disappointed if we stick to the method outlined above.

Let us suppose that the bird in question is prepared to learn. If he is you will soon notice that he is glad when the lesson begins. He will even begin to read the words from one's lips, so to speak. He will not merely learn to say short sentences, he will even be able to recite a nursery rhyme or whistle a song, and he will never leave you in any doubt as to his feelings when he considers himself neglected. As soon as he does he will begin to call, and he will not desist until you come up to him and give him some of your time. There is no doubt that such a bird provides a lot of fun for a long time.

We shall now consider how to tame and turn into a well-behaved pupil a young bird already out of the nest. The disadvantage we have to make up for is the fact our pupil has probably been flying about with his kind for a time and has picked up a fair amount of the usual Budgerigar language. As soon as we separate him from the others, he is apt to look very sad. In fact, he will probably refuse to have anything to do with us for a day or so.

On the other hand, we must see that he is not left alone. We should try to attract his attention, and the best way of doing this is to give him food after having left him without it for approximately four hours. As soon as he gets hungry and notices our putting a vessel of seed into his cage, he will become interested in spite of himself. When he has eaten his fill, however, we take the vessel away again and repeat this for some time. Then we try and get a little more intimate. We keep the vessel in our hand and wait for him to conquer his fear. After some time, he will come and cautiously pick a seed, after which he will turn round and scuttle away again. In time, he will get used to this, and there is certainly no need to cut his wings unless, after a week, he still keeps flying off to hide away on the top of some cupboard where we cannot reach him. In that case, we have to rob him of some of the power of flight by clipping the ends of six consecutive feathers of one wing. After this operation he will still be able to fly, but not to get out of reach. We should not attempt to take him into our grip, if we can avoid it, as even a completely tame Budgerigar has objections to this. We then try and get him to perch on a stick we hold out to him. From there we pass on to our finger and, in this way, gradually gain his confidence.

In his cage, we may fix a swing and a climbing-pole. He is certain to use both a lot during the day. And if we can let him fly free for some time every day, so much the better. If he does, it will not take long for him to come and share our table at meals!

There is always danger when a bird is flying loose. We shall have to do without a cat, but a dog will get used to the bird so quickly that there is no cause for alarm there. However, if we happen to leave a window open and the bird flies off, we shall probably have seen the last of him. His flight is so swift he will be far away before he knows what is happening, and unlike the larger parrots that, as a rule, will not fail to find their way back, Master Budgie will be lost so completely that only good fortune can save him.

With this method, as with the first, talking lessons must wait until the bird becomes completely tame. This will take much more time but, on the other hand, we shall have saved a few troublesome weeks by starting this much later.

The tame Budgerigar's ability to learn tricks derives from his playfulness and his love of gymnastics. A swing and a climbing-pole are his pet pieces of furniture. When we make a long rope ladder and hold it out to him he will scale it at once. If we hang the rope ladder

over the table he will scale it on one side and descend on the other. Our bare hands are enough to teach him to climb. When he is sitting on one finger we hold another finger over it, then another and still another. In this way he will learn the trick in a jiffy. Sitting at the end of a stick, he is overjoyed when the stick is swung around, raised, lowered and so on. That is probably how he was conditioned to riding in toy motor cars or even on the engine of a toy train and on various other kinds of automatic vehicles. A fireman's truck with a ladder offers a wealth of possibilities and it really seems that the bird himself relishes this kind of thing.

PART TWO

BREEDING

11. COLOUR CHARACTERS

No doubt some Budgerigar fanciers are satisfied with a good knowledge of the many different colour varieties which exist today. To them the question of how these colours come into being or how they can be propagated and combined is of little interest. On the other hand there are a great many breeders who are exceptionally keen to know just how colour inheritance operates so that they can successfully produce the many colour forms. I shall endeavour to explain as clearly as possible how colour characters are inherited and why colour forms can be bred by the breeders as and when they wish. Most breeders of Budgerigars will, I feel certain, find the production of many of the colour varieties of tremendous interest and others will of course specialize in one form.

The present-day laws that govern the inheritance of Budgerigars are based on the principles that were discovered by Gregor Mendel (1822–1884) during his research work on plant inheritance. It is interesting to note that practically everything that is written today on the subject of Budgerigar genetics starts from the experimental work carried out by Dr. H. Duncker and General Consul C. H. Cremer of Bremen working upon Mendel's findings. Dr. Duncker's theories were tested and proved in Britain by such experimental breeders as Elliott, Weston, Rattigan, Wall and Rogers. Later, the further researches in colour inheritance made by Dr. Steiner of Zurich and Prof. F. A. E. Crew of Edinburgh added still further to the knowledge of the colours of Budgerigars. For explaining the various colour characters several different formula have been used quite successfully, but for simplicity's sake it is not intended to trouble the breeder with these in the course of this book. For those who are interested in genetic formula I recommend *Genetics for Budgerigar Breeders* by Taylor and Warner (Iliffe Press), now out of print.

Before I proceed with any further details of the principles of hereditary as evolved by the pioneer experimental breeders there are several points which must be explained in detail. One of the foremost of these that the breeder must always have in mind is that although a pair of birds may be of one colour (phenotype) they can produce other colours if they are of an impure genetical make-up (genotype). In all breeding experiments it is therefore absolutely necessary to know the true and correct pedigrees of the parent birds used before the theoretical expectations can be properly calculated. Each breeding pair must breed under strict control with only one pair in each cage or pen.

The various hereditary characters which include size, shape, type, etc., as well as the colours, are carried on microscopic bodies known as chromosomes which are in pairs, except for those controlling the sex. Each half of a pair of chromosomes has a different set of genes, and it is these genes which actually control the various hereditary characters. When a pair of Budgerigars mate, the cock's sex cell carrying half a set of chromosome pairs combines with the hen's egg cell also containing half a set of chromosome pairs, thereby forming a completely new whole set of chromosomes.

I will now explain how this controls the colours produced by each individual breeding pair of Budgerigars; for instance, if we take a pure Sky Blue cock and mate him to a pure Light Green hen all the resulting youngsters they produce will be light green in colour like their mother. However, they will not be of the same genetical make-up, as they have inherited half a set of chromosomes from each parent. The cock bird's half set contains the genes for producing blue colour whereas the hen's half set contains the genes for green colour. As the green genes are Dominant to the blue ones all the young ones are therefore green in colour but carrying hidden the potential for blue colour. If, on the other hand, each member of the pair had been mated to its like colour, the cock bird would have given only Blue chicks and the hen bird only Green ones.

Now let us see what happens to the impure young ones they have produced, and such birds are known in the Budgerigar Fancy as Light Green 'split' Blue. All impure birds are described by putting their visual colour first, followed by an oblique stroke thus '/' (or split mark) and then their hidden colour or colours. When two of these Light Green/Blue birds are mated together they will produce in the usual Mendelian ratio of 1:2:1. In other words, 25% of the chicks will be pure Light Greens like their grandmother, 50% Green/Blues like their parents and 25% pure Sky Blues like their grandfather. There is no visual way to identify the pure Light Greens from the ones that are 'split' for Blue and this can only be discovered by test pairings. During the early part of the experimental work in colour breeding a very large number of matings similar to the one mentioned above were made and the results carefully tested. It was interesting to note that the percentages worked out very accurately even though individual nests and pairs of birds gave very varied results. In all experimental work the percentages can only be calculated on the collated results of many pairings of the same kind. The various colours operate in exactly the same manner as those indicated above, and in later chapters we shall see just how these various pairings reproduce. Once the breeder has mastered the methods of calculating pairings it should be reasonably easy to forecast the results from any given pair providing they are not of a too complex nature.

We have just seen how the simple Dominant and Recessive characters operate, but this is not the end of inheritance as there are further characters to be considered. When it comes to the inheritance of the different shades of varieties a special formula is used for what is known as incomplete dominance. It is well known that with each different colour and variety there are three shades governed by the Dark character. This Dark character is not an actual colour in itself but one that alters the depth of other shades. In the case of the Light Green the Dark character is absent, and with the Dark Green it is present in single strength, but with the Olive Green it is there in double strength. Therefore when an Olive Green is mated to a Light Green all the young they produce are dark green in colour. This shows that the Dark character is only incomplete in its Dominance because if it had been fully dominant all the young would have been Olive Greens. Now when two Dark Greens are mated together we again get the simple Mendelian ratio of 1:2:1—that is, Light Green, Dark Green and Olive Green. This same ratio of the Dark character inheritance operates all through the different colours and varieties and is quite independent of other characters that may be carried by the breeding pairs. The following table will show just how the Dark character operates and can be applied to any pairing. To make this clear I will call the double quantity of Dark DD, the single quantity Dd and the absence dd.

1. DD × DD will give 100% DD.
2. DD × dd will give 100% Dd.
3. Dd × Dd will give 25% dd, 50% Dd and 25% DD.
4. Dd × dd will give 50% dd and 50% Dd.
5. dd × dd will give 100% dd.

Having these simple methods of inheritance clearly in mind the next fact to discover is the difference in the Dominance and Recessiveness between the various colour forms. All colours of Budgerigars can be divided into two groups—those with the yellow ground and those with the white ground. A further variation is the strange pale whitish-yellow colour produced by the Yellow-faced character, but this must be included for the time being in the Blue group.

The wild type Light Green Budgerigar is Dominant to all other colours and from it stems all the various and complex green shades, to mention a few—Olive Green, Light Yellow, Greywing Dark Green, Fallow Olive, Slate Light Green, Opaline Dark Green, etc., etc. The Recessive Blue series contains such birds as Mauve, White Sky Blue, Greywing Cobalt, Fallow Mauve, Slate Sky Blue, Opaline Cobalt, etc., etc. Within each group of colours some are Dominant to others; for instance, in the Green series Light Green is Dominant to Greywing Light Green, Greywing Light Green is Dominant to Light Yellow, Light Yellow is Dominant to Fallow Light Green, and a similar thing happens with the Blue series. Any pure member of the Green series mated to any member of the Blue series will always give all green-coloured young. In addition to straightforward cross-pairings which give quite simple expectations there are certain much more complex ones where several characters are carried by each parent. When such birds are mated together a very interesting colour range of youngsters can be produced and we will go into this more closely in later chapters.

In addition to the normal mode of inheritance as outlined in the previous paragraphs there is the sex-linkage inheritance which is to be found with five of our varieties. I think that it would be as well to explain how sex-linkage operates before we proceed further. The varieties which are controlled by sex-linkage are the Opaline, Slate,

Cinnamon, Albino (and Lutino) and the red-eyed Lacewing. The theoretical expectations for these varieties can all be calculated by using the following formula:

(i) Sex-linked cock × sex-linked hen will give all sex-linked young.
(ii) Sex-linked cock × non-linked hen will give all non-linked/sex-linked cocks and all sex-linked hens.
(iii) Non-linked cock × sex-linked hen will give all non-linked/sex-linked cocks and all non-linked hens.
(iv) Non-linked/sex-linked cock × sex-linked hen will give sex-linked cocks and hens, non-linked/sex-linked cocks and non-linked hens.
(v) Non-linked/sex-linked cock × non-linked hen will give non-linked cocks and hens, non-linked/sex-linked cocks and sex-linked hens.

When two different kinds of sex-linked birds are used one of them acts as though it were a non-linked bird; for instance, if a Cinnamon cock was mated to an Opaline hen the result would be as in (ii) above, although the cock birds would be 'split' for both of the sex-linked characters.

When it comes to mating certain colours in the single Dark series there is a variation in the result of the actual shade of colouring of the young produced, although they do divide quite nicely into the blue and the green groups. For quite a time breeders were a little puzzled why certain Dark Green/Blue birds produced many of the Cobalt series whereas others having the same visual colour produced very few indeed. After examining the results and pedigrees of a considerable number of these Dark Green to Sky Blue pairings it was discovered that with certain birds the Dark character was linked more closely with the Blue than in the others where the Dark was linked with the Green. The examination of these results shows that with one kind of Dark Green/Blue known as Type II the theoretical expectation is 43% Cobalt, 7% Sky Blue, 43% Light Green/Blue and 7% Dark Green/Blue. The opposite type known as Type I gives an expectation of 43% Sky Blue, 7% Cobalt, 43% Dark Green/Blue and 7% Light Green/Blue. It will be seen from this that it is quite easy to distinguish by the breeding results which birds belong to each type. This difference applies to the whole of the Dark Green/Blue series irrespective of what other colour characters are carried by the birds in question.

In addition to the Dark character, which causes a change in the depth of shade, there are two other characters which also effect a variation in the shade of the colours, including birds having the Dark character. They are the Australian Dominant Grey and the Violet characters, both of which are Dominant in their manner of inheritance, and birds can have the character in either a single or double strength with the same visual effect. The Grey character masks the other colours, giving in the Green series a dull clear olive shade which is variable in depth according to the Dark character. When Blue series birds have the Grey character they assume a clear grey shade, again varying in depth according to the Dark character they may carry. There can be a Grey form of all the other varieties and many very interesting types can and have been bred. The Violet character again alters the shade of colour carried by the Blue series birds so that a Sky Blue plus the Violet character appears to the eye as a pale bright cobalt shade. When the Cobalt and Violet combine the beautiful visual Violet results, and when Violet and Mauve come together the Violet Mauve comes into being. There seems to be some evidence to show that when birds have the Violet character in double strength their visual colouring is a little more solid than it is when only in single strength. This difference in shade depth is also controlled to some extent by the actual shade of the Blue series to which the Violet has been added. Although it may seem a little odd, it is possible to have the whole series of Green birds with the Violet character, and they are known as Violet Greens. The fact that Green birds can have particular character which causes visual Violets to appear is in fact a shade altering colour similar to that of the Grey. There can be a Violet form of all the other colours and varieties, including the Greys and Slates.

In addition to the various shades of colouring there are also several different pattern mutations such as the Opaline, the Clear-flighted, the Clearwing, the Spangle, the (Danish) Recessive Pied and the Dominant (Australian) Pied, all of which can be had in the whole range of colour forms each showing their individual pattern markings.

The following points should always be borne in mind by breeders, and these are that it is not possible for any coloured bird to carry in 'split' form a Dominant colour character. It is also not possible for *any hen* bird of any colour or variety to carry a sex-linked character in 'split' form, and this must always be remembered when calculating expectations. It would seem that there is one exception to the ordinary rules of inheritance in the Dark-eyed Clear series which result in a combination of the Dominant Clear-flighted and the Recessive Danish Pied characters. These birds are perfectly clear yellow or white throughout with the dark plum-coloured eyes of the Danish Recessive Pied. However, when they are mated to pure normals, they will give some Clear-flighted young. So it would seem in actual fact that the Dark-eyed Clears are the Danish Recessive Pied form of the Dominant Clear-flighted which gives perfectly clear birds. I will have more to say about these later on.

12. THE NORMAL VARIETIES

In the last chapter I discussed the ways in which some of the colour characters of Budgerigars are transmitted and will now develop the theme. Budgerigars are roughly divided into two categories—the Normals and the rare colours; however, the line of demarcation is very fluid at the present time, so readers must forgive me if I term what they may think a rare colour an ordinary normal.

We have seen that the wild type Green from which all colours have been evolved is Dominant to all others, and this is what one would expect. We have also discovered that with each Green and Blue series there can be three shades of colouring due to the presence or absence of the Dark character. This has been explained so the breeder will now know when certain colours are mentioned just where they fit in the rules of Dark inheritance.

The breeding of the wild type or normal Greens is quite straightforward and Light Green to Light Green gives only Light Green young with, of course, the very remote possibility of a mutation. Whilst on this point I must say that it is always possible to get a mutation either an existing one or a brand new one from any pair of birds at any time. The recorded cases of genuine mutations are extremely few, and most cases of the unexpected appearance of odd colours can be explained by the birds being of mixed parentage. However, should any unusual colour appear in a nest which the breeder cannot identify, the opinion of an experienced fancier should be sought, just in case it may be something new.

In the Green series probably the Dark Green is the most interesting to breed as when two such birds are mated together they produce all three Green shades, i.e. Light, Dark and Olive Green. Because of the incomplete Dominance of the Dark character, Dark Greens can never breed true when mated together, but the Light Greens and Olive Greens from these matings can do so. When two Olive Greens are paired together all their young are Olive Greens and are quite pure, and the same remarks apply to Light Greens.

The Recessive form of the Light Green is the Light Yellow, and here again they can exist with three different depths of body shade and, in addition, there is also a very big variation in their purity of colour. From the exhibition point of view good Light Yellows are clear yellow throughout showing only the faintest of ghost markings on their wings. On the other hand there are Light Yellows that show a strong green suffusion on their bodies and quite visible markings on their wings. These birds are still Light Yellows in the true sense, although they may not answer to the exhibition standards. In addition to the ordinary Light Yellows there are Dark Yellows and Olive Yellows, the former having one Dark character and the latter two.

The Dark Yellows and Olive Yellows are two very interesting groups and are not bred very freely these days and therefore offer quite a good field for new breeders to carry out experiments in colour purity. If the Dark Yellows and Olive Yellows could be produced on the same lines as the exhibition Light Yellow type some very richly coloured birds could result.

When Light Yellows are crossed with Light Greens all the resulting young are light green in colour but 'split' for Yellow. Two of these Light Green/Yellows mated together gives the familiar Mendelian ratio 1:2:1 of Light Yellow, Light Green/Yellow and Light Green. The Dark character can be included in the scheme and the colours will work out in exactly the same ratio but with the added variation of the Dark character as outlined in the last chapter.

The next normal variety we will take is the Greywing Light Green; these birds are not as one might first suppose the result of crossing together Light Yellows and Light Greens, but are a distinct mutation. The Greywings are Recessive to the normal Light Greens and, when crossed, all the young are Light Green/Greywing. When paired to Light Yellows they assume the role of the Dominant and they produce all Greywing Light Green/Yellows. Breeders will be interested to note that if a Light Green/Greywing is mated to a Light Yellow the same colour result is obtained as if a Greywing Light Green were used. This indicates that the Greywing is Dominant to the Light Yellow and at the same time it is not possible for a normal Green bird to be 'split' for both Greywing and Light Yellow. There can, of course, be all three shades of Greywing Greens, and the calculations can be worked out on the same lines as those of the Green series.

An interesting and rather fascinating result can be obtained by crossing Greywings with a related group known as Clearwings, or in the case of the green birds Yellow-wing Greens. We have seen that when Greywing is paired to Light Yellow all the resulting young are Greywing Light Green/Yellows. When Yellow-wing Light Green is paired to Light Yellow all the resulting young are Yellow-wing Light Green/Yellows, all quite straightforward and simple. Now when Greywing is mated to Yellow-wing something quite unusual happens as the resulting young are a combination of both characters in the one bird. The young from this cross are known as full body-coloured Greywings as in fact they have an almost full normal body colour with the usual grey wings. When such birds are mated to Light Yellows they give 50% of each kind, i.e. 50% Yellow-wing Light Green/Yellow and 50% Greywing Light Green/Yellow, showing clearly that they are a combination of both of these characters.

If we take the yellow colour from the normal Light Greens we have the Sky Blues which occurred as a separate mutation many years ago. Like their Light Green counterparts two pure Sky Blues paired together will give only Sky Blue young. When the Dark character is added the single quantity produces the beautiful Cobalts and the double quantity the more sombre Mauves. Here again the Cobalts are probably the most interesting from the breeding angle as when two are paired together they give all three shades in the usual percentages. If all Cobalt birds are required it cannot be achieved by mating together two Cobalt parents, but it can be done by mating Sky Blues to Mauves. Such pairings will give all Cobalt young, and in fact it is the only way in which this result can be achieved. Should Cobalts be mated to Mauves both colours will result in equal proportions.

The Blue counterparts of the Light Yellows are known as White Sky Blues and were evolved in the first place by crossing Light Yellows with Sky Blues, thereby producing the double Recessive in the second generation. The White Sky Blues are like their Light Yellow counterparts and vary greatly in their purity of colouring, although on the whole they are more inclined to show a medium to a heavy suffusion rather than a clear white body. They, too, can be had in the three suffusions, and many lovely birds result from adding the Dark character, thereby producing White Cobalts and White Mauves.

Greywing Sky Blues can be easily evolved by introducing the Blue character to the Greywing Light Greens. This can be achieved in two ways—either by the use of normal Sky Blues or White Sky Blues. If

Greywing Light Greens are crossed with normal Sky Blues the resulting young are Light Green/Greywing Blues. Two of these 'split' birds mated together will give a percentage of both Greywing Greens and Greywing Sky Blues. If one of these Light Green/Greywing Blues is mated to a normal White Blue then a much larger percentage of Greywing Sky Blues will result, all these birds will be 'split' White, of course. On the other hand, if Greywing Light Greens are mated to White Sky Blues, all the resulting young will be Greywing Light Green/Whites, and when mated back to further Whites will produce both Greywing Light Green/Whites, Greywing Sky Blue/Whites as well as normal Light Yellow/Whites and White Sky Blues. The Greywing Blue series can be had in all the three depths of body shade making quite a nice collection.

It is still a moot point whether or not the Grey series and the Violet series can be considered among the Normals, and this is a point which has to be watched when it comes to the question as to which classes certain birds should be entered at an exhibition. There can be a Grey form of all the normal Greens and the normal Blues, including the Greywings, Whites and Yellows. The same thing applies to the Violet shades, but here there is a little difference because of the variation in the shade. When the Grey character is added to the Green birds it produces a Grey Green colouring varying in depth according to the variety to which it has been added. When added to the Blue series a similar thing happens and the birds have a graduated grey shade. Now with the Violet character it is only one particular group of birds, the Violet Cobalts, that show the visual Violet shade in their plumage. All the other birds having the Violet character show a variation in their colouring but do not appear to the eye as Violets. The Green series can also have the Violet character in their genetical make-up, but the birds themselves are still of a green shade even though it may be an unusual one. I will have more to say about the production of the Violet character birds and how they are produced in a later chapter. Both the Grey and Violet characters are Dominant and it is not possible for any coloured birds to carry them in 'split' form.

Illustrations: Plates 1–12, 14–16.

13. YELLOW-WINGS AND WHITEWINGS

(The Clearwing Group)

The Clearwing group of Budgerigars comprises of the varieties known as Yellow-wings and Whitewings in the whole range of different body colours and is a definite and separate mutation and must not be confused with normal Yellows and normal Whites showing a heavy body suffusion. Genetically they are Recessive to the normal Green and Blue series (including the Fallow group), but Dominant to the ordinary Yellows and Whites. With the Greywing character they combine and form a further visual type—the full body-coloured Greywings of which I will have more to say later.

As their group and individual names indicate, the birds of this mutation should have either yellow wings or white wings with their body colours as near as possible to the normal depth of colour according to the variety to which they belong. For example, a perfect Yellow-wing Light Green would therefore have clear yellow wings, head and neck, and a light green body and appropriate matching tail. As it would be expected, extremely few birds come within reach of this perfection. It is the desire of their breeders to improve the exhibition strains for colour, type and size, and to this end a specialist association has been formed in Great Britain under the name of The Clearwing Budgerigar Breeders Association. Under the guidance of this Association and the Budgerigar Society the general standard of the group has been greatly improved and many of these beautifully coloured Budgerigars are now bred and exhibited.

All the various normally coloured forms of the Clearwing group reproduce in the same way, and once the breeder has mastered their method of inheritance in one colour the expectations from others can easily be calculated.

We have seen that the Clearwing character is Recessive to the normal and therefore any normally coloured bird can be 'split' for Clearwing. We also know that the Clearwing character is Dominant to the ordinary Yellow and White birds and naturally Clearwings can be 'split' for these colours. There is a very important point regarding these birds which must always be borne in mind, and that is it is not possible for any normally coloured bird of any colour to be 'split' for both Clearwing and Yellow (or White). This knowledge will be of great value to the breeder when testing normal birds to see if they are 'split' for Clearwing. If a Light Green is paired to a Light Yellow and gives only Light Green and Light Yellow young it can be considered as definitely *not* being 'split' Clearwing. On the other hand, another bird of the same visual colour paired to a Light Yellow which gives Light Green and Yellow-wing Light Green young is a definite 'split' Clearwing.

Yellow-wings or Whitewings can have either a single or double quantity of the character without any visual difference in their external colouration, the difference lies only in their breeding potential.

Some theoretical examples will I think make this fact more clear to breeders. If a Yellow-wing Light Green, double factor, is paired to a Light Yellow it will give all Yellow-wing Light Green/Yellow young, whereas if it had been 'split' for Yellow, then half of the young would have been Yellow-wing Light Green/Yellow and the other half ordinary Light Yellows. When two Yellow-wing Light Green/Yellows are mated together they will give a theoretical expectation of 25% pure Light Yellow, 50% Yellow-wing Light Green/Yellow and 25% pure Yellow-wing Light Green. This of course is the usual Mendelian ratio that can always be expected from such a combination. If on the other hand the pair had consisted of two Light Green/Yellow-wings, then the theoretical expectation would be 25% pure Light Green, 50% Light Green/Yellow-wing and 25% pure Yellow-wing Light Green. A similarly coloured result would have been obtained if one of the parent birds had been a Light Green/Yellow-wing and the other a Light Green/Yellow. From such a mating the genetical make-up of the young produced would be quite different, and they would consist of Light Green, Light Green/Yellow, Light Green/Yellow-wing and Yellow-wing Light Green/Yellow.

The Whitewings reproduce in exactly the same way as their Yellow-wing counterparts and like them they can carry the character in either a single or double quantity. As an example, a Whitewing Sky Blue paired to a White Sky Blue will produce all single factor birds, i.e. Whitewing Sky Blue 'split' for White. When one of these birds is paired to a White Sky Blue they will give 50% Whitewing Sky Blue/White and 50% White Sky Blue.

When a Whitewing Sky Blue is paired to an ordinary Sky Blue all the young are Sky Blue/Whitewing, and if paired to normal Whites will produce Sky Blue/Whites and Whitewing Sky Blue/Whites. The Dark character operates in the normal way and there can be all three shades of blue in the Whitewing series.

We have seen how the Yellow-wings and Whitewings reproduce themselves and that they follow the normal method of inheritance. When it comes to reproducing the best coloured birds it is generally thought that Yellow-wing Greens (or Yellows) should always be crossed to Whitewing Blues (or Whites) so that the brilliancy of the colour is maintained. At the same time it is important to select each member of the pair for their good points of shape, size and type, in addition to their colouring. The birds selected for breeding purposes should have wings as clear as possible and at the same time having as deep a breast colouring as can be found among the stock. If one of these characters is not particularly good on a bird it is always best to select the purest wing colour even at the expense of the depth of breast colour.

Some very handsome Whitewing birds can be produced in all three body shades by including the Yellow-faced character in their make-up, thereby producing Yellow-faced Whitewings. The Yellow-faced character can be introduced either via Yellow-faced normal Blue series birds or the less common Yellow-faced White series. If, say, a Yellow-faced (single factor) Sky Blue is mated to a Whitewing Sky Blue, the young will be Sky Blue/Whitewing and Yellow-faced Sky Blue/Whitewing. If one of the latter is mated to a Whitewing Blue or White Blue then 25% of the young will be the desired Yellow-faced Whitewing Sky Blue. There is, however, one snag about the introduction of the Yellow-faced character to the Clearwing strain and that is it tends to make the markings on the wings deeper than required in this particular variety. However, it may be possible by many years of careful selection to breed Yellow-faced Clearwings that really do have purity of wing colour.

In addition to the three normal shades in each of the Clearwing series it is possible to produce them with Grey, Grey Green, Violet, Violet Green, Slate and Slate Green body colours. These unusually coloured varieties are mostly bred by experimental colour breeders but occasionally specimens of them do appear on the show benches from time to time.

A further interesting form of Clearwings can be evolved by the use of the Opaline character which results in the Opaline Clearwings in both the Green and Blue types. These birds have an intensely brilliant body colour with the characteristic opaline markings on their wings, and this is of the same shade as their body, giving an overall effect with some specimens of 'Self'. These 'Self' birds are very handsome and intense in their colour, and although they have naturally lost the Clearwing characteristic this is made up by their bright clear mantle and blue- or green-coloured markings on wings. With a little care and a few generations of selection, these 'Selfs' can be evolved, but of course during their production numerous birds will result which are only half-way to the desired colour. All the Blue series birds have a further use, if the breeder so desires, in helping to produce 'Rainbows'. See Chapters 14 and 22 for further details of these brightly coloured composite birds.

Illustrations: Plates 13, 17, 35.

14. THE YELLOW-FACED BLUE SERIES

Prior to the Yellow-faced Blue mutations it was always thought that Budgerigars could not be bred having both yellow- and white-coloured areas on the same birds. The appearance of the Yellow-faced Blue mutations in several parts of the world at approximately the same time gave most breeders a pleasant surprise. As Yellow-faced Blue birds increased, it soon became apparent that several different forms were in existence and that they had distinct yet similar colour patterns. These Yellow-faced Blue characters can be carried by all the Blue series birds in either single or double quantities, although the majority of the birds seen today are of the single factor kind.

At the present time two separate kinds of Yellow-faced birds have been identified and recognized, they are known as the Mutant I and Mutant II kinds, and other forms and combinations are known but have not yet been fully investigated. All the Yellow-faced characters are Dominant to the Blue series but naturally Recessive to the Green. The Mutant I Yellow-faced birds show the yellow colouring on face, wing butts and tail, with occasional overspill near the bib, and these are much desired for exhibition purposes. The Mutant II kind show much more yellow suffusion and in some specimens it spreads completely over the body giving a peculiar sea-green colour effect. In certain lights and with some specimens it is extremely difficult to tell such birds from ordinary Green ones and this has led to misunderstandings. With the Mutant I kind a rather strange thing happens when double factor birds are bred. These double factor birds have white faces and appear to the eye to be just ordinary normal blue birds. However, when paired to true normal Blue birds, all the young they produce have yellow faces and are, of course, single factor Yellow-faced Blues. This phenomena mystified breeders for some years until it was clarified by a series of articles that appeared in *Cage and Aviary Birds* contributed by Matt Bender, Dr. J. Eugene Fox, Prof. G. T. Taylor, C. Warner and C. H. Rogers.

It would seem from observations that with the Mutant II type the birds carrying the double factor may even be more heavily suffused with the green overlay than those with only a single factor. Most breeders only produce single factor birds of both kinds as it is usual to mate Yellow-faced birds to normal Blue series so that 50% of each is obtained. This practice is carried out to a great extent by the desire of breeders to improve the general overall quality of their stock, and this is best done by the use of first-class normal birds.

There can be a Yellow-faced form of all the existing Blue series birds, and this includes the Fallow, Slate, Red-eyed, Dark-eyed Clear and Pied kinds and many beautifully coloured birds can and have been evolved by enterprising breeders. Perhaps one of the most intensely coloured of the Yellow-faced composite types is the Yellow-faced Opaline Clearwings, more commonly known in the Fancy as 'Rainbows' because of their brilliant and varied colouration. 'Rainbows' are obtained by combining the Opaline, Clearwing and Yellow-faced characters in one bird, and there are many different matings that will give this combination in varying percentages. A few examples are given below, all of which have been tried by various breeders.

1. Opaline Whitewing Sky Blue cock × Yellow-faced White Sky Blue hen.
2. Whitewing Sky Blue/Opaline cock × Yellow-faced Sky Blue/White hen.
3. Yellow-faced Whitewing Sky Blue/Opaline cock × Whitewing Sky Blue hen.

Of course the varying shades of blue can be included in these matings and other matings and they add further to the variation of the 'Rainbows' ultimately produced. 'Rainbows' can be had in all the different depths of colouring, including the Greys, Slates and Violets, but it is generally the Sky Blue, Cobalt, Violet Sky Blue and Violet Cobalt forms that are considered to give the best overall colour effect. Of course in their production some of the other shades are produced, and they, too, can be used advantageously for producing 'Rainbows' of the desired colours. Wherever possible it is best to avoid using the Grey character as the birds produced, even though they have the complete combination of characters, are quite dull and do not answer strictly to the name of 'Rainbow'.

The Yellow-faced characters can be carried by all the Green series birds and breeders frequently use such specimens to improve the general overall quality of the Yellow-faced kinds ultimately produced. As it would be expected, such birds appear to the eye as ordinary Green series types, and their special qualities can only be discovered by breeding or the owner's knowledge of their pedigrees.

These Green series birds which carry the Yellow-faced character in their make-up and the very heavily green suffused Yellow-faced birds have in the past mystified breeders because of the way they have produced Yellow-faced young quite unexpectedly. As I have already pointed out, the heavily suffused Yellow-faced birds can always be detected by the blue colouring under their wing butts. Such birds will, of course, produce only Yellow-faced and Blues when paired to Blue series birds, even though they themselves do appear to be 'Greens'. Green birds carrying the Yellow-faced character will always prove mysterious until the breeder has fully realized the method of transmission of this particular character.

In addition to the Yellow-faced forms just discussed there also exists more than one form of birds that have an extremely deep golden yellow face and are generally known as Golden-faced Blues. There can be a Golden-faced form of all the existing blue coloured birds. The breeding behaviour of these Golden-faced birds is somewhat different to that followed by the Yellow-faced Mutant I and II forms. When a Golden-faced Blue having two characters for this colour in its genetical makeup is paired to an ordinary Normal all the resulting young are Golden-faced Blues with a single character. Although these birds have the characteristic bright golden face their body is heavily suffused with a yellow overlay. With the Golden-faced Blues having the *double character* this heavy overlay is absent leaving the yellow face deep clear and bright. When two of these single character Golden-faced Blues are paired together they reproduce in the normal Mendelian ratio 1 : 2 : 1, that is to say 25% Normals, 50% single character Golden-face and 25% double character Golden-face. This method of colour reproduction was discovered by K. H. Gray of Tiptree, Essex who has bred both Yellow-faced and Golden-faced birds for many years. It is also thought that like the Yellow-faced characters there exist several different Golden-faced forms.

Illustrations: Plates 38–43.

15. THE FALLOWS

It is now known that at least three different breeding forms of Fallows exist, each exhibiting the same general body colouring and wing markings. The very first Fallow mutation that was reported occurred in America, but unfortunately it was not established at that time, and it was many years before they appeared again as a mutation in that country. The first established strain of Fallows was in Germany, and from there they rapidly spread to all parts of the world and were known as German Fallows. Some years after this strain was fully established another race of Fallow birds appeared in England and were naturally named English Fallows. Although both of these birds had very similar colouring throughout they were recognizable through the difference in the colour of their eyes. The German Fallows have red pupils surrounded by light iris rings whereas the English Fallows have brighter but solid red eyes. It is therefore quite a simple matter to distinguish between these two strains by just looking at the colour of their eyes. Other Fallow types have occurred as mutations in Scotland, Australia, South Africa and America, but their relationship to the two well established types is not yet completely unravelled.

Although it is quite simple to distinguish between most of the German and the English Fallow varieties by the colouring of their eyes recent experiments by the Editor have brought to light an interesting contradiction. When the Danish Recessive Pied character is introduced into a German Fallow strain the resulting German Fallow Recessive Pieds that are produced show the characteristic pied pattern markings with the Fallow colouring. The strange thing about these birds is that the colour of their eyes is bright clear red without the light iris ring and appears to the eye to be the same as English Fallows. The young normal Fallows in the same nests as these Fallow Recessive Pieds have the ordinary German Fallow eye colour.

A fact that has surprised many breeders from time to time is when a German Fallow is paired to an English Fallow all the resulting youngsters are birds with normal black eyes, although both of their parents have red eyes. Such birds carry the character for both kinds of Fallow, and when paired to either kind will give Fallow young of that particular kind.

The tables which govern the inheritance of Fallows are quite straight-forward and can be used to calculate the results of either kind of Fallow but not when they are mixed.

Fallow inheritance

1. Fallow × Fallow gives 100% Fallow.
2. Normal × Fallow gives 100% Normal/Fallow.
3. Normal/Fallow × Fallow gives 50% Normal/Fallow and 50% Fallow.
4. Normal/Fallow × Normal/Fallow gives 25% pure Normal, 50% Normal/Fallow and 25% Fallow.
5. Normal/Fallow × Normal gives 50% Normal/Fallow, 50% pure Normal.

Although Fallows are not bred very widely in this country these days a number of specimens are produced each year and find their way to the shows where they are always a subject of interesting discussion amongst Budgerigar breeders.

Fallows are, I think, rather fascinating birds to breed, and some quite intriguing combinations can be created with a little ingenuity on the part of their breeders. By combining Fallow, Yellow (or White), and Cinnamon, it is possible to produce birds that have the appearance of being either Lutinos or Albinos as their eyes are red and their colour is a clear yellow or clear white throughout. These 'synthetic' Albinos and Lutinos produced great interest when they were first bred and many quite experienced Fanciers were puzzled by them. It is now some years since this type has been bred, but they can always be recreated at any time given the necessary birds. Of course, if the Yellow-faced character is added to the 'synthetic' Yellow-faced Albino, the Yellow-faced Cinnamon Fallow White is evolved.

Another intriguing form of Fallow can be manufactured by combining the Fallow, Opaline and Grey characters, and this can be done in both the German and English Fallow series and, of course, with both the Green and Blue types. This combination will give the Fallow

Opaline Grey or Fallow Opaline Grey Green kinds. The former birds have an almost white body, very lightly marked head and neck and brownish-grey markings on wings. With the latter the body colour is almost pure yellow with similar markings. Both of these types are interesting to breed and will give the keen breeder much satisfaction when they are produced. Such birds have sometimes been called Clearbodies which they are in actual fact, but they must not be confused with the true American Clearbody mutation.

I think that perhaps the most pleasing colour of the normal Fallows is the Fallow Olive Green, the body colour of these birds is a beautiful rich golden-orange yellow shade which is not to be found in any other variety. Unfortunately, only very few of these birds are seen today, but their numbers could soon be increased if any breeder wishes to cultivate this kind. If, for instance, the breeder has, say, a Fallow Light Green, then it can be paired to a normal Olive Green which will result in all Dark Green/Fallows being produced. Such birds mated together will give 25% Fallows of which a small proportion will be of the desired Fallow Olive Green. Once a few specimens have been obtained it is quite easy to increase and improve the quality of the birds. Because of the shortage of Fallow breeding stock with breeders having only the odd bird Albinos or Lutinos have been used at times as mates because they too have red eyes. Such matings however are not good for increasing Fallow strains because of the masking effect of the Albino (Lutino) character. Unless some special experiment is to be made it is always advisable to pair Fallows, both the German and English kinds, to good quality pure Normals.

As readers will have realized, there can be a very wide range of Fallows, and that anyone interested in genetical problems will find their production extremely rewarding, particularly so as their red eyes make them stand out even when first hatched. It is often very nice to know whether or not you have produced the desired colour as soon as the chicks arrive without having to wait until they have completely feathered.

Illustrations: Plates 23, 24.

16. THE VIOLET CHARACTER

It is, I think, generally accepted by Budgerigar breeders everywhere that among the violet-coloured birds will be found the most brilliantly coloured specimens of our Budgerigars. The character we all call Violet is one that alters the body shade of every variety and all colours in both the Green and the Blue series, However, it is only when combined with certain other colour characters, namely, Blue and Dark, that the true vivid visual violet shade is produced. In all other combinations of factors where the Violet character is present it results in only a change of colour tone.

It is very important for breeders to remember that the Violet character is a Dominant one and as such it is not possible for any normally coloured bird to have the character in 'split' form in its genetical make-up. Even normally coloured birds that are bred from one or even two Visual Violet parents are no different genetically than those bred from two ordinary normals. The idea that certain birds could be 'split' for Violet originated, I think, before the full knowledge of the transmission of the character was known and understood by breeders. It was thought at one time that Visual Violets were a separate colour, and when visual Violet birds appeared in nests from pairing certain dark-blue-coloured birds bred from one Visual Violet parent and a normal Cobalt or Mauve or Mauve birds from similar matings paired to normal Blues, that these Violet bred birds were actually 'split' for Violet. In due course it was discovered that both Sky Blues and Mauves could have the Violet character in their make-up and that it made a difference to their visual tone of colour. As all the Green series can have the Violet character, this too made breeders think that these birds were 'split' for Violet.

The Violet character being Dominant means that all and every colour and variety can be produced in a Violet form, but it is only those birds which also have the Blue character, a single Dark character, and a single or double Violet character that are visible Violet birds.

The mechanics of Violet inheritance are really quite straightforward and will soon be seen when the table below is studied:

1. Violet (s.f.) Sky Blue × Mauve gives 50% Violet (s.f.) Cobalt, 50% Cobalt.
2. Violet (d.f.) Sky Blue × Mauve gives 100% Violet (s.f.) Cobalt.
3. Violet (s.f.) Sky Blue × Cobalt gives 25% Violet (s.f.) Cobalt, 25% Violet (s.f.) Sky Blue, 25% Cobalt, 25% Sky Blue.
4. Violet (d.f.) Sky Blue × Cobalt gives 50% Violet (s.f.) Cobalt, 50% Violet (s.f.) Sky Blue.
5. Violet (s.f.) Sky Blue × Sky Blue gives 50% Violet (s.f.) Sky Blue, 50% Sky Blue.
6. Violet (d.f.) Sky Blue × Sky Blue gives 100% Violet (s.f.) Sky Blue.
7. Violet (s.f.) Cobalt × Sky Blue gives 25% Violet (s.f.) Cobalt, 25% Violet (s.f.) Sky Blue, 25% Cobalt, 25% Sky Blue.
8. Violet (d.f.) Cobalt × Sky Blue gives 50% Violet (s.f.) Cobalt, 50% Violet (s.f.) Sky Blue.
9. Violet (s.f.) Cobalt × Cobalt gives 12½% Violet (s.f.) Sky Blue, 25% Violet (s.f.) Cobalt, 12½% Violet (s.f.) Mauve, 12½% Sky Blue, 25% Cobalt, 12½% Mauve.
10. Violet (d.f.) Cobalt × Cobalt gives 25% Violet (s.f.) Sky Blue, 50% Violet (s.f.) Cobalt, 25% Violet (s.f.) Mauve.
11. Violet (s.f.) Mauve × Sky Blue gives 50% Violet (s.f.) Cobalt, 50% Cobalt.
12. Violet (d.f.) Mauve × Sky Blue gives 100% Violet (s.f.) Cobalt.
13. Violet (s.f.) Mauve × Cobalt gives 25% Violet (s.f.) Cobalt, 25% Violet (s.f.) Mauve, 25% Mauve, 25% Cobalt.
14. Violet (d.f.) Mauve × Cobalt gives 50% Violet (s.f.) Cobalt, 50% Violet (s.f.) Mauve.
15. Violet (s.f.) Mauve × Mauve gives 50% Violet (s.f.) Mauve, 50% Mauve.
16. Violet (d.f.) Mauve × Mauve gives 100% Violet (s.f.) Mauve.

The above tables can be used in calculating the expectations of any particular variety of bird containing the Violet character or any mixtures of these characters and Violet. It will be clearly seen that the character is a Dominant one, but it is only expressed as a Visual Violet when the necessary characters are together in one bird. In actual fact a Violet Sky Blue or a Violet Mauve is equally as much a Violet as the well-known Visual Violet (Violet Cobalt), to give them their correct name. It will be seen from the tables how visual Violet birds can be produced without either parent showing the true Violet character. In fact the most satisfactory way of getting all Visual Violet young is to mate either a Violet Sky Blue (d.f.) to a normal Mauve or a Violet (d.f.) Mauve to a normal Sky Blue. Where single factor birds are used then 50% of the young will be Visual Violets.

It is extremely difficult to give the exact colouring of Violet Sky Blues as these vary with individual strains, much depending on the kind of Sky Blues used in the production. As we all know, Sky Blues vary quite considerably in the depth of their colouring, and undoubtedly the deeper birds are better for the ultimate production of the Violet shades. When it comes to the Violet Mauves it is again a little difficult to identify all of these birds, although generally speaking they do show distinct flecks of violet colouring particularly on their thighs and rump and the general colour is less leaden than in most normal Mauves.

When the Grey character is combined with the Violet character the resulting birds are of a soft warm mauve tinted grey shade. The cheek flashes are very dark and dull, but the two long tail feathers remain black. There can be hight, medium and dark shades of Violet Greys.

As it has already been stated, there can be a Violet form of the whole of the Green series, and it is possible to get green-coloured birds having the Violet character in their make-up and yet to all intents and purposes are pure Greens. The Violet character in such cases has acted as the Grey character does in the Grey Greens. We all know that it is possible to get Grey Greens that are not 'split' for Blue but nevertheless they still carry the Grey character. The same form operates with the Violet Green birds, but of course there are not a great many in existence, because breeders invariably mate Violet carrying Greens to Blue series birds. It has been found during the course of experimental pairings that the use of Green series birds in the production of Visual Violets is beneficial in improving and maintaining the desired depth of colour.

With regard to the actual colouration of the Violet Green series, the Violet Light Greens are a pale dark green with a slight yellowish underflue. The Violet Dark Greens are a very solid dark green colour much deeper than the normal Dark Green and again has frequently this yellowish cast. Although only very few of the Violet Olive Greens have yet been bred, they are nevertheless extremely handsome birds and very dark and level in their colouring. All these Violet Green shades are definitely more even and sounder in tone than one would imagine and particularly with the Dark and Olive Green birds.

As I have already said, there can be a Violet form of all the known varieties and colours, and it can be imagined that some very beautifully coloured birds can be evolved by including the Violet colour character in their genetical make-up. Violet Clearwings, Violet Opalines, Violet Cinnamons, Spangles, Violet Dominant Pieds and Violet Recessive Pieds all have their own particular beauty, and the more one sees of these colours the more desirous they become. I feel sure that as Budgerigar breeding progresses more Fanciers will be adding the Violet series to their stocks whether they keep birds for exhibition purposes or just for their own particular beauty.

The following theoretical examples can be used as a guide for breeders who wish to introduce Green colour into their Violet strains to help to enrich the colour of the visual Violets ultimately produced.

1. Violet (s.f.) Cobalt × Light Green/Blue gives $12\frac{1}{2}\%$ of each of the following colours—Violet (s.f.) Cobalt, Cobalt, Violet (s.f.) Sky Blue, Sky Blue, Violet Dark Green/Blue, Dark Green/Blue, Violet Light Green/Blue and Light Green/Blue.
2. Violet (s.f.) Sky Blue × Dark Green/Blue gives $12\frac{1}{2}\%$ of each of the following colours—Violet (s.f.) Cobalt, Cobalt, Violet (s.f.) Sky Blue, Sky Blue, Violet Dark Green/Blue, Dark Green/Blue, Violet Light Green/Blue and Light Green/Blue.
3. Violet (s.f.) Mauve × Light Green/Blue gives 25% Violet (s.f.) Cobalt, 25% Cobalt, 25% Violet Dark Green/Blue, 25% Dark Green/Blue.

Illustrations: Plates 10, 61.

17. RECESSIVE DANISH PIEDS

The first race of true Pieds to be established in Great Britain were the Recessive Danish Pieds. The original stock came to England from Herr C. af Enehjelm of Finland who sent two breeding pairs to C. H. Rogers, then of Cambridge. From this original nucleus the majority of the birds of this type seen in Great Britain today originated. A few further specimens were imported when the ban on Parrot-like birds was lifted for a short time in 1952. There have lately been further importations of these Pieds since the ban was again lifted.

This particularly attractive form of Pied can be had in every other variety and colour and, of course, the very numerous combinations. However, it is generally accepted by the Fancy that the Pied forms of the normal type give the best results. The pattern markings of the Recessive Danish Pieds vary very considerably, although the majority
Recessive Danish Pieds vary very considerably, although the majority
body with some dark markings spotted over their wings, back of neck and head. The normal throat spots are sometimes entirely absent and other specimens will carry one or two or three visible spots on each side. The cheek patches themselves are invariably of two colours—silver and the normal violet colour. The feet and legs are always flesh-coloured, and the eyes, a distinguishing feature, are a deep solid plum colour throughout without the usual light iris ring.

As their name indicates, their method of reproduction is a Recessive one and a Recessive Danish Pied paired to any other colour will produce only normally coloured young all of which will be 'split' for Recessive Danish Pied. The following rules govern the inheritance of this particular character and can be applied to any of their colours of forms.

1. Recessive Danish Pied × pure Normal gives 100% Normal/Recessive Danish Pied.
2. Recessive Danish Pied × Normal Recessive Pied gives 50% Recessive Danish Pied and 50% Normal Recessive Pied.
3. Normal Recessive Pied × Normal Recessive Pied gives 25% pure Normals, 50% Normal Recessive Pied and 25% Recessive Danish Pied.
4. Normal Recessive Pied × pure Normal gives 50% Normal Recessive Pied and 50% pure Normal.

5. Recessive Danish Pied × Recessive Danish Pied gives 100% Recessive Danish Pied.

There is no way of visually distinguishing between the pure Normals and those 'split' for Recessive Danish Pied. In certain cases 'split' birds will show a small clear spot on the nape of their neck, and at one time breeders thought this was a sure way of distinguishing 'split' birds. However, this is definitely not the case, and a bird carrying this small mark can be either 'split' or pure. It is thought that this tick marking was introduced into the strain in the very early days when a normal cock bird showing this particular marking was used by C. H. Rogers to pair into his strain of Recessive Danish Pieds.

It was some years after the introduction of Recessive Danish Pieds before any real progress was made in developing birds having the desired exhibition points. Nevertheless, some beautifully coloured specimens in many colours were bred up and down the country and undoubtedly helped to popularize these Pieds. The exhibition side was helped very much by the formation of The Pied Budgerigar Society of Great Britain, a specialist body catering solely for the various Pied forms. This Society formulated coloured standards for the Recessive Danish Pieds and all other Pieds, and this gave breeders a better idea as to what was required in exhibition birds. The real progress was made when, after careful research work, it was discovered that Recessive Danish Pieds could be improved from the exhibition angle by only using first cross 'split' normals to pair with Recessive Danish Pieds. It was seen that these first cross 'split' birds, bred from the best quality normals paired to selected Recessive Danish Pieds, gave equally as many Pieds and birds of better quality than the 'splits' bred from many generations of Pied crosses. First cross 'splits' are bred by pairing Recessive Danish Pieds to pure Normals.

It had been discovered that the continual pairing of Recessive Danish Pieds to Recessive Danish Pieds resulted in a loss of substance and a reversion to the original type. At the same time the colour areas of some of the birds produced from these pairings were greatly reduced and some specimens carried as little as 5% overall dark markings. These light birds seem to be mainly cock birds, whereas the hen birds, strangely enough, are inclined to show too much dark. As with all matings of every colour, selection of the initial stock birds is of great importance, and this applies to both the Pied and the non-Pied birds used for breeding Pieds.

Many of the normal Grey series have very good show properties and have been introduced to the Pied strains, including the Recessive Danish Pieds. This has resulted in many cases in the loss of brilliancy of colour which has always been associated with Recessive Danish Pieds. If the breeder is going to use Grey series birds of first-rate quality to mate to Recessive Danish Pieds they should only be used periodically and wherever possible the normally coloured birds from these pairings should be used in preference to the Grey series.

It will be realized of course that some very beautifully coloured Pieds can be created by the use of the Violet, Cinnamon and Opaline characters and, of course, their combinations, and these can be multiplied further by the inclusion of the Yellow-faced character. These other characters operate in exactly the same way as they do when used in the normal crosses.

At one time it was thought by some breeders that the use of Albinos or Lutinos in Pied strains would help to produce better colour, but breeding results have proved this to be entirely wrong. In addition to the general colour not being improved, the introduction of Albinos or Lutinos produced birds having these characters and thereby masking the desired Pieds. It is therefore not advisable to use any of these red-eyed kinds as mates for Recessive Danish Pieds, and for that matter any of the other Pied kinds. The use of ordinary White and ordinary Yellow birds as mates for Recessive Danish Pieds again results in the production of the Pied forms of these birds which are not attractive because they lack colour contrast.

Without a doubt, the most satisfactory and best looking Recessive Danish Pieds are those of the ordinary normal types, and these of course can include the Violet and Yellow-faced series. There are considerable possibilities for improving and maintaining the Recessive Danish Pieds in the forms mentioned above. As with all Recessive varieties a constant watch must be kept on every breeding pair to see that they are matched to give the maximum good results.

NOTE. Recessive Danish Pieds are the same as Recessive Pieds.

Illustrations: Plates 44–48.

18. CONTINENTAL CLEAR-FLIGHTED AND DUTCH PIEDS

For a long time birds having varying amounts of clear areas on their plumage were bred on the Continent, but it was not until somewhere about 1940 that a clearly defined race of Clear-flighted birds was evolved in Belgium. Good well-marked specimens of these Clear-flighted birds are very distinct and cannot be mistaken even by the novice breeder. Their characteristics are a clear spot at the nape of neck, completely clear flights and long tail feathers, their bodies, wings, etc., are coloured according to the variety to which they belong. It can well be imagined that with such a pattern marked variety there is certain to be a big variation in the markings among individual birds and strains. The ideal birds are as I have just described, and they may be bred from many different pairings, providing one member of the pair has the Clear-flighted character. This character is definitely Dominant, and a Clear-flighted bird with a single character will produce both Clear-flighted and Normals when mated to a Normal. It would seem that it is far easier to produce well-marked cock birds than it is hen birds, and in fact many hens show only the Clear-flighted character by a clear spot at nape of neck. These birds are equally as much Clear-flighted as the well-marked specimens and can even breed perfectly marked birds, although the chance of this is quite small.

The Clear-flighted character being a Dominant one is carried with the same visual effect in either single or double quantities, but no other colour can carry it in 'split' form. However, it can be masked both by the Albino and Lutino forms and, of course, by the Dark-eyed Clears, about which I shall have more to say in a later chapter. As would be expected, there can be a Clear-flighted form of all the members of the Green and Blue series, including the Yellow-faced kinds. Generally speaking, it is the ordinary normal forms of the Clear-flighted that give the best coloured results because of the clear cut contrast. With some of the forms, particularly the more pallid kinds, the Clear-flighted character does not show itself to advantage.

Nevertheless, some very interesting specimens carrying a combination of various characters can be evolved, and will give the breeder much enjoyment in their production.

Individual breeders have their own ideas as to the best way in which to produce the ideally marked birds, and I think this is partly due to certain strains having their own slight breeding peculiarities. During the course of experiments it has been discovered that selection of the parent birds plays an important part in getting the maximum number of well-marked birds. In numerous cases it has been seen that when a Clear-flighted cock that is reasonably well marked is mated to a hen having only the characteristic clear head spot, the resulting young are usually good and many may be perfect or nearly perfectly marked. Being a Dominant variety they are more simple to improve than the Recessive kinds, and if first-class Normals are selected as the initial mates, some really good exhibition birds can be evolved.

It would seem that one of the greatest failings with Clear-flighted birds is the breaking of the colour on the chest so that the mask overspills some distance on the chest. In addition to this some birds show patches of colour on their wings and neck. At one time these broken patterned examples were thought to be Dutch Pieds, a variety which appeared in England during the early fifties, and seemed to be mainly evolved from a single example that was imported into this country from Holland—the exact origin of the bird was not actually discovered. The difference between these Dutch Pieds and the broken patterned Clear-flights is that, with the former, it is just as easy to breed hen birds as it is cocks. Only a few of these Dutch Pieds now exist, and some of them have been crossed with broken patterned Clear-flighted birds and it is difficult to find pure specimens. Nevertheless, odd examples appear occasionally and find their way on to the show benches where they are exhibited along with all the other kinds of Dominant Pieds. It should be added here that the Dutch Pied character is Dominant and can be had in single or double quantities both in cocks and hens with the same visual colouring. The general colouring of the Dutch Pieds is 50% Dark and 50% Clear areas with the pattern broken evenly and spread over the whole bird. Some very nice examples have been bred both in the Green and Blue series, including Opaline and Cinnamon kinds. Another difference between these and the Clear-flighted is that with the latter the colouring on the wings may be a little grizzled, but this is not so with the Dutch kind.

Owing to the scarcity these days of the Dutch Pieds there has been very little experimental work with the variety and it is not known if when crossed with the Recessive Danish kind they would produce dark-eyed clear birds in the second generation.

During 1972 the Editor made an investigation into the possible number of true Dutch Pieds now in existence in Great Britain. After examining a considerable number of various Pied birds showing different degrees of pied markings he could not find a single specimen that could be recognised as a genuine Dutch Pied. It is therefore thought that there is every possibility of the strain now ceasing to exist in this country.

Going back to the production of Clear-flighted birds it should be noted that throat spots are essential with this variety, and all exhibition specimens should have a full set of these together with unbroken cheek flashes. It is the throat spots, together with the evenness of pattern markings, that make these birds so attractive in the decorative aviary and on the show bench. Breeders who are interested in this pattern breeding are well advised to add Clear-flighted birds to their stocks. Being a Dominant they can be crossed with Normal and do not in any way affect the purity of any normally coloured birds they produce. In other words, the breeders need not fear having 'split' birds among their pure strains

Illustrations: White-flighted, Plate 36 (Australian) Plate 37.
Yellow-flighted, Plate 57 (Australian) Plate 58.

NOTE. Dutch Pieds are the same as Dominant Pieds.

Illustrations: Plates 49–52.

19. THE DARK-EYED CLEAR WHITES AND DARK-EYED CLEAR YELLOWS

Until the sudden appearance of the Dark-eyed Clear kinds, breeders had for many years tried to produce birds that were quite pure in colour and free from any kind of markings. Their efforts had met with a certain amount of success when the Cinnamon forms of the ordinary Whites and Yellows were bred. Although some of these birds showed promise they still had some suffusion and ghost markings on their plumage which selection could not eradicate. Even the red-eyed Albinos and Lutinos showed degrees of suffusion on their rumps and flanks when viewed in certain lights and particularly so in artificial lighting.

The appearance of the Dark-eyed Clears was welcomed by breeders, but it was quite a long time before the actual formula for their production was unravelled.

Dark-eyed Clears are quite pure in the Yellow or the White colour they have, and no vestige of suffusion or markings of any kind can be seen in any lights in their plumage. Their eyes are a solid, dark plum colour without the light iris ring—hence their name—which is designed to distinguish them from any race that may appear in the future that have the ordinary normal black eyes.

The first Dark-eyed Clears were produced in aviaries where Danish Recessive Pieds and Dominant Continental Clear-flighted birds were allowed to breed freely together. From this it was discovered that these two very different breeding kinds of Pieds somehow combined to give birds that were pure white or pure yellow in their whole colouring. In due time it was found that Dark-eyed Clears could be bred by pairing Continental Clear-flighted to Danish Recessive Pieds and then pairing the resulting Clear-flighted young back to Danish Recessive Pieds. This is all very simple where the precise pairings are known, and if so the Dark-eyed Clears can be bred to order and many breeders are finding this a simple Mendelian exercise. However up to date, the reason just why the combining of two different Pied kinds should give some birds that are perfectly clear has not been satisfactorily solved.

Dark-eyed Clears can mask any colour, so that a Dark-eyed Clear White could be a Dark-eyed Clear form of a Mauve or a White Blue, but would appear exactly the same to the eye. With the Dark-eyed Clear Yellows, which again can mask any variety, the colour that is actually masked does have a certain bearing on the actual tone of the yellow. For instance, a Dark-eyed Clear masking normal Olive Green is deeper and richer in shade than, say, one that is masking Light Yellow. There can of course be a Yellow-faced form of the Dark-eyed Clear White which again can vary in colour according to the type of the Yellow-faced character used in their production.

The pairings that govern the breeding of Dark-eyed Clears are quite straightforward and simple to apply and the most used ones are as follows:

1. Clear-flighted (single factor) × Recessive Danish Pied gives 50% Clear-flighted Recessive Pied, 50% Normal Recessive Pied.
2. Clear-flighted (double factor) × Recessive Danish Pied gives 100% Clear-flighted (single factor) Recessive Pied.
3. Clear-flighted (single factor) Recessive Pied × Recessive Danish Pied gives 25% Recessive Danish Pied, 25% Normal Recessive Pied, 25% Clear-flighted (single factor) Recessive Pied, 25% Dark-eyed Clear.
4. Dark-eyed Clear × Recessive Danish Pied gives 50% Dark-eyed Clear, 50% Recessive Danish Pied.
5. Dark-eyed Clear (single factor) × Dark-eyed Clear (single factor) gives 50% Dark-eyed Clear (single factor), 25% Recessive Danish Pied, 25% Dark-eyed Clear (double factor).
6. Dark-eyed Clear (single factor) × Dark-eyed Clear (double factor) gives 50% Dark-eyed Clear (single factor) and 50% Dark-eyed Clear (double factor).

There are, of course, a number of other crosses that will give varying percentages of Dark-eyed Clears. The composition of the Dark-eyed Clears themselves can differ which, of course, affects the percentages they produce. It will be seen from pairing No. 5 above that two Dark-eyed Clears can actually produce Recessive Danish

Pieds if the parent birds are of a certain combination of characters. The percentage is given as 25% Danish Recessive Pieds, but although this may work out over a large number of pairings, it may not work accurately in single matings. It has been my own experience that with Dark-eyed Clear pairings only Dark-eyed Clears have resulted, whereas other breeders have produced both Dark-eyed Clears and Recessive Danish Pieds. This result is no doubt due to the fact that at least one of the Dark-eyed Clears used by myself was a double factor bird. A pairing of a double factor to a single factor will give only Dark-eyed Clear young.

From the results I have seen up to date, the best type and most substantially made Dark-eyed Clears have resulted from the mating of selected Recessive Danish Pieds and Clear-flighted 'split' Danish Recessive Pieds. I think that it is yet far too early to mate Dark-eyed Clears together as they are still only in the process of being evolved as exhibition birds.

As far as it can be discovered the Fallow form of the Dark eyed Clears has not yet been bred mainly because of the scarcity of suitable breeding stock. Such birds would have red eyes, clear yellow or clear white colouring throughout, and would look like Lutinos or Albinos without any suggestion of suffusion on flanks or rump. The production of this composite form would be a worthwhile exercise for keen colour breeders.

Illustration: Plate 59.

20. DOMINANT AUSTRALIAN PIEDS

The appearance of the Australian Pied type in competition with the already established Recessive Danish Pieds started the popularity of the Pied kinds in Great Britain. The competition between the two kinds stimulated interest and, with the help of The Pied Budgerigar Society of Great Britain, they were standardized and their general colouring and type improved. The first Australian Pied mutation appeared in Sydney somewhere about 1935, but it was not until the late fifties that specimens arrived in England. From information received it seems that the first specimens were recognized and selected from a batch of mixed coloured Budgerigars and mated to good quality exhibition type stock. At that time very little was known in this country of their hereditary behaviour except that they were thought to be Dominant. Owing to their attractive colouration and their apparent willingness to reproduce their kind their numbers quickly multiplied. With the increased numbers available breeders quickly got to work and many experimental crosses were tried. Unfortunately, during these initial experiments, such varieties as Albinos, Lutinos, Red-eyed Lacewings, Whites, Yellows and Recessive Danish Pieds were crossed in with the Australian Pieds with the result that many Pieds today carry undesirable 'split' characters and in some cases they have inherited the pattern markings of the Recessive Danish type.

It was eventually ascertained that the character that causes this particular kind of Pied is definitely a Dominant, and consequently birds can carry the character with the same visual effect in either single or double quantities as is usual with a Dominant character. The majority of the Dominant Australian Pieds are single character birds because in their production breeders have repeatedly crossed them with first-class normal stock. This continual out-crossing has resulted in many typical exhibition type birds being produced in quite a wide range of colouring. The Dominant Australian Pieds are roughly divided into two kinds, those which are known as the Banded (like the original mutant), and those which are of heavily broken colouring which are classed as Australian Dominants.

Without a doubt a well-marked Banded Pied of one of the normal colours is a very beautiful bird indeed and must on account of its colouration command admiration. These Banded Pieds are coloured as their normal counterparts but carry a head spot, all clear flights and tail, and a clear band across the middle of their chest. As would be expected only a very limited number of perfectly marked birds are produced each season, but there are many more which closely approach the ideal. One of the outstanding features which I feel sure appeals to many breeders is the fact that the good show specimens have a complete set of throat spots and unbroken cheek flashes.

The rules that govern the inheritance of the Dominant Australian Pied character irrespective of their actual colour are governed by the following:

1. Dominant Australian Pied (single factor) to pure Normal gives 50% pure Normal and 50% Dominant Australian Pied (s.f.).
2. Dominant Australian Pied (double factor) to pure Normal gives 100% Dominant Australian Pied (s.f.).
3. Dominant Australian Pied (single factor) to Dominant Australian Pied (s.f.) gives 25% pure Normal, 50% Dominant Australian Pied (s.f.), 25% Dominant Australian Pied (d.f.).
4. Dominant Australian Pied (s.f.) to Dominant Australian Pied (d.f.) gives 50% Dominant Australian Pied (s.f.), 50% Dominant Australian Pied (d.f.).
5. Dominant Australian Pied (d.f.) to Australian Dominant Pied (d.f.) gives 100% Australian Dominant Pied (d.f.).

It should be specially noted that any normally coloured birds arising from pairs covered by rules 1 and 3 are exactly the same as normal birds bred from any pure normal crosses.

Although the rules of inheritance shown above indicate exact percentages when it comes to actual individual pairings there may well be quite a diversity in the actual results. It should be realized that when percentages of any matings are calculated they are done so over a very large number of different pairings of the same combinations. I have known some cases where Dominant Australian Pied single factor mated to a Normal have produced up to nine or ten normal young and only one or two Dominant Australian Pieds. In other cases just the reverse has happened, and it has been nearly all Dominant Australian Pieds that have been bred. In one particular instance an Dominant

Australian Pied Light Green cock mated to a Light Green hen produced two nests of five Dominant Australian Pieds in one year, and the following year the first nest of four were all Dominant Australian Pieds. In the second nest of the second year the young were five normal Light Greens. I have mentioned this just to show how variable individual matings can be and how easy it is to jump at wrong conclusions by not having sufficient material.

Breeding results show clearly that it is best to produce Dominant Australian Pieds by mating them always to first-quality pure Normal birds. By this method the general quality of colouring, substance and type are steadily improved. It will be noted that I have made emphasis about pure Normals as I feel that this is so important in producing the correctly coloured Dominant Australian Pieds. Earlier on in this chapter I mentioned about Dominant Australian Pieds inheriting the colour pattern of the Recessive Danish type. This has been brought about by the use of both Recessive Danish Pieds and Normal birds 'split' for that character as mates for the Dominant Australian Pieds. These Dominant Australian Pieds produced from such matings show definitely Recessive Danish Pied characteristics, such as broken cheek flashes, incomplete sets of throat spots and markings usually considered applicable to the Danish Pied type. It will be realized that such birds are difficult to recognize and also have lost a great deal of value as exhibition birds. In nests where both Dominant Australian Pieds and Recessive Danish Pieds appear it is often difficult to distinguish between the youngsters, and many birds have been incorrectly named and disposed of just because they were bred from one Dominant Australian Pied parent. However, when these youngsters become adult they can be clearly distinguished by their different eye colourings—the Australians having the normal dark eyes and the Danish the solid plum-coloured eyes.

As with all pattern-marked birds, it is essential to select each pair, and wherever possible the Dominant Australian Pieds mated to Normals should show a strong leaning towards the Banded type, and if this procedure is followed the percentage of the right coloured birds will steadily increase.

As I have already remarked there can be an Dominant Australian Pied form of all the other colours and varieties and some very handsome birds can be evolved. Once again I would warn breeders against the use of Recessive Danish Pieds, Albinos, Lutinos, ordinary Yellows and Whites, and in most cases Opalines, as mates for Dominant Australian Pieds. I have said that Opalines should not be used in the majority of cases, but at times an Opaline can be used to introduce certain essential features that it may possess and are needed in the Dominant Australian Pied strain. The use of the other colours mentioned will I think only lead to disappointments in later pairings. Without these varieties there are still plenty of other kinds that can be and are used most successfully in breeding some wonderful specimens of the now so popular Dominant Australian Pied Budgerigars. Recently a few birds have been bred of the Dominant Pied kind of poor quality colour being mainly clear with very few dark areas and have odd coloured eyes, one eye being the normal dark with light iris ring and the other deep solid plum colour without the iris ring. Such birds could possibly be Bi-coloured Pieds or a further extension of the Recessive Pied character being displayed by the Dominant kind.

Illustrations: Plates 53–56.

21. THE CRESTED TYPES

Towards the end of the nineteen-thirties a type of Budgerigar having a distinct crest on the head appeared as a mutation in North America. It was found that this Crested variety could be produced in all different colours and that the Crest character was a Dominant one. For some long time these birds were only few in number, but gradually they spread to Europe and finally Great Britain. It is also thought that other Crested mutations have occurred and that these have been crossed in with the original American type. It is here in this country where most of the experimental work on the development of the Crested Budgerigars has been carried out under the auspices of The Crested Budgerigar Club. It is through the efforts of this Club that standards of perfection for the Crested birds have been evolved and are now used at the principal exhibitions.

There are three distinct types of crests recognized in the exhibition series—the Tufted, the Half-circular and the Full-circular, with the latter being the most sought-after form. As it has already been mentioned it was quickly found that the Crested character was a Dominant one but other agents were also connected with their reproduction. The original breeders found that only a limited number of Crested birds were produced by their pairings and it is only quite recently that the position of the Crested character has been made much more clear and the results now fit into a given breeding pattern. Before going into the breeding behaviour in more detail it should be noted that in addition to the birds desired for show purposes specimens have been produced carrying more than one crest. Some of these birds seem to have a crest in the normal place and another crest on the lower part of the head or even on the back of the neck or mantle. Although these particular birds do not appear very frequently it is said they are of great value in producing good types of Normal Crested birds.

A recent theory that has been put forward several times to account for the small number of Crested birds that appear from certain crosses with pure normal birds is that these latter have characters in their make-up which prevent the crested character from being expressed fully. From such matings a few Crested birds do result together with a large number of non-crested birds, and these latter are now known as Crestbred. When Crested birds are mated to Crestbred Normals then the percentage of Crested birds produced rises quite sharply. This is, of course, quite in line with the breeding behaviour of other Crested kinds such as Crested Canaries and Crested Bengalese.

The number of Crested Budgerigar breeders in this country are, of course, limited at the present time, and consequently the number of test pairings are likewise limited. As the number of breeders increase so the amount of reliable data from controlled pairings is building up. All this information seems to point strongly to this fact that Crestbred Normals are much more useful than ordinary straight Normals. In fact I believe there is on record a case where two Crestbred birds actually produced Crested young ones. As the majority of the Crested birds seen these days lack in substance it will still be very necessary to use pure Normals for cross-mating to improve general substance and type. It has not yet been established whether or not Crestbred birds with a long crested parentage are more useful than the first-cross Crestbreds. It would seem to me that the first-cross birds are the best type to use as they must carry more good quality characters than the other Crestbred types. Up to the present time breeders have been generally experimenting with their Crest pairings and trying to produce different colours with crests and this has meant there has been only slow progress in the improvement of substance. Now that there are available a number of reasonably sized birds with very good crests of the three types, breeders are paying more attention to the development of good exhibition crested birds. This improvement has been noticeable at some of the larger shows held recently, and it would seem that there is every possibility of more and better Crested Budgerigars appearing in the very near future.

Among the more recent thoughts on the Crested inheritance it has been suggested that there is a lethal factor to be contended with. This, of course, is well known with the breeding of the Crested Canary types, and evidence seems to point strongly to this being also effective with Crested Budgerigars. The recorded breeding results, although somewhat limited at the present time, do seem to indicate that there may be a lethal factor at work when two Crested birds are paired together. Before this is definitely established many more matings will have to be made, recorded and analysed. At the present time breeders usually pair one Crested to a pure Normal or a Crestbred Normal, and this is the main reason why so few Crested to Crested pairings are available for analyzing.

The latest theory on the inheritance of the Crested character is that in addition to this character which manifests itself in three different forms there are inhibiting factors which govern the appearance of Crests. The evidence gathered from quite a wide range of matings both in this country and abroad seems to support this fact, but here again there must be a considerable quantity of other matings taken under control before the final answer is achieved.

The presence of these inhibiting factors does not deter from the fact that the Crested character is a Dominant one, but it can be altered by the presence of these factors. A bird actually showing a crest possesses two of the Crested characters, whereas a bird with only one character, i.e. a Crestbred, does not show the character because of its possession of an inhibiting factor. Such a factor would prevent the crest from showing visually, although in actual fact the bird does possess the character which in its double form makes a crest visible. There may be several of these inhibiting factors at work and this would account for the crest being expressed in its three different forms, i.e. Circular, Half-circular and Tufted. Bearing this in mind it will be seen that there can be quite a number of different genetical formulas which give different visual and hidden expressions of the Crest character.

So as not to confuse the newcomer to Crest breeding it is best to suggest to them that the Crest is a Dominant character and when paired to a pure Normal produces Crests and normal-looking birds. The numbers of Crests which are actually produced from such crossings will in most cases be small, but in the light of the theory of inhibitors mentioned above it will be understood more clearly. When these normal-looking birds bred from one Crested parent, now commonly called Crestbreds, are mated back to Crests, the number of actual Crests produced is substantially increased. If the breeder follows this pattern of mating when selecting the breeding pairs the results will be in keeping with the usual Crested inheritance.

As the breeding of Crested Budgerigars progresses and the size and shape of the crests are improved by selection, I feel sure that the above suggested theory will be seen to be the one which answers the question of Crested inheritance.

In the 1985 edition of the Handbook of the Crested Budgerigar Club the Inhibitor Theory of crest inheritance is fully explained, together with the results of different pairings between Crests and the several kinds of Crest-breds.

In addition to the original mutation from North America there appears to be a further one that originated on the Continent of Europe, and although there is a slight variation in the placing of the feathers between these two mutations, they can be crossed together quite satisfactorily without causing too much complication. It is very probable that the fact that two mutations exist and have been mixed together accounts for the variation in the breeding results of certain matings. I have mentioned the fact about the two mutations because breeders may wonder why in certain cases their Crested birds vary somewhat in the actual formation of their Crested feathers.

Illustrations: Plates 66–68.

22. NEW ESTABLISHED VARIETIES

Spangles

In 1978 reports reached Great Britain that a new variety had been established in Australia, named Spangles because of their very distinctive wing markings. They had first appeared in several different breeding establishments somewhere about 1975, and being Dominant their numbers were quickly multiplied. Examples of these attractive birds came to Great Britain in the early 1980s and fine examples are now appearing at many of the large Cage Bird Exhibitions.

They can be had in all the Green and Blue series varieties, except Inos and Dark-eyed Clears, and their markings are similar to those of Spangled Poultry varieties. The main features of their colouring are mask white (yellow), throat spots black often with a white (yellow) centre, cheek flashes and body colour similar to their normal counterparts, wing markings each feather edged with black, flight and tail feathers also edged with black. Their method of inheritance is Dominant but rather unusual as it is only birds that have a single Spangle character which actually show the attractive pattern markings; with double character birds the wing markings etc are virtually absent.

Saddle-back

A further mutation was reported in Australia soon after the Spangles, and was called Saddle-back because of its distinctive colour pattern. It was suggested that the first specimens were just poorly marked Opalines but further breeding dispelled that idea. Saddle-backs differ from the sex-linked Opalines, being Recessive. This means that the Saddle-back character can be carried in split form by other varieties. Another difference is that the characteristic clear bar on the leading primary wing feathers and the Opaline wing colour are absent. Although these birds are now breeding in some Continental aviaries they have not yet arrived in Great Britain.

23. SOME OTHER VARIETIES

In addition to the varieties mentioned in the foregoing chapters there are some others which at the present time do not enjoy very much popularity and have not yet been standardized. In addition to these there are some composite types which, although not actual varieties, do appear in various Budgerigar publications under given names. These we will discuss at the end of this chapter.

A variety with a sex-linked inheritance that first appeared in England in 1943 was called the Slate because of its slate-like colour. In actual fact Slate is similar to the Violet character because there can be a Slate form of all the other kinds of Budgerigars. Slate acts as a character which alters the tone of the colour of the bird which has in addition Slate in its genetical make-up. If Slate is added to, say, Sky Blue, then a Slate Sky Blue is produced, and such a bird would be marked similarly to a normal Sky Blue, but its body colour would be a clear light slate shade with the cheek flashes a darker and duller violet and the tail feathers correspondingly a darker blue. If a Slate is added to Light Green then the Slate Light Green is evolved, and here the bird would have the same markings as the Light Green but with a pale yellowish dark-green body shade with the cheek flashes a darker and duller violet and the tail feathers correspondingly a darker blue.

The Slate variety went out of popularity when the Dominant Australian Grey made its appearance in Great Britain. There is a similarity between the two mutations and as the Grey is Dominant in its manner of inheritance it appealed to breeders much more than the sex-linked Slate. At one time it was thought that the Slate had disappeared, but in the late 1940s a few specimens were discovered in the aviaries of various breeders, mostly in the Opaline form. Since that time breeders have been trying to produce the normal types of Slates, and they found it very difficult to separate the two sex-linked mutations, but nevertheless in the end they succeeded. Now that more fanciers are producing Slates a much better type of bird is being evolved, and at some of the recent National exhibitions Slates have won their sections. The Slate character is reproduced in exactly the same way as the Cinnamons, Opalines, Albinos and Lutinos. Once the breeder has mastered the method of sex-linked reproduction of one kind it can easily be applied to any other sex-linked form.

Another sex-linked variety which came into being during the late 1940s is the Red-Eyed Lacewings which can be had in all the known colour patterns. Because of their peculiar colouration the birds can only be produced in three kinds of body colours, namely, yellow, white and the yellow-faced white shade. The depth of markings varies quite considerably with the birds that have normal Green counterparts being the darkest and those having the normal Yellow counterparts the palest. In actual fact the latter birds are very difficult to distinguish from ordinary Lutinos and can quite well be mistaken for them by breeders not well acquainted with Lacewings. There can be Pied forms, Clear-flighted forms and Opaline forms in all three shades, giving quite a large range of wing patterns. The colouration of a Lacewing Light Green is head, neck, back and wings, clearly marked with pure cinnamon brown with the tail feathers being a deeper shade and the body a clear yellow with a slight suffusion on thighs and rump. The actual depth of yellow varies with the Light, Dark and Olive Green kinds. With the Blue series there is of course only one body shade, and that is white again with a faint suffusion on thighs and rump.

Although not generally popular at the present time, Lacewings have found favour with some breeders who like a sex-linked variety that is different from the ordinary Albinos and Lutinos and have definitely improved the general appearance of their stock. It has been found that the use of the Grey and the Violet character in the production of Lacewings is most advantageous and some quite credible birds both for colour, substance and type, have been bred by the use of these additional characters, particularly the Grey. Without a doubt Lacewings provide a good scope for breeders who are interested in developing a pastel shaded sex-linked variety.

From time to time odd birds have appeared with similar markings to the Lacewings but with normal dark eyes. Unfortunately this form has not been established in Britain although they seem to have appeared and been established in Australia under the name of Greywing Yellows. As these birds have not been seen here little can be said about their precise colour markings. The odd feathers and wings which have been sent over show the birds to be as described—that is, having greyish wing markings and more or less yellow body colours. It has been the aim of some breeders in this country to try and evolve this type from badly coloured specimens of the true Greywings, but little success has been achieved so far.

Within the last few years reports have come from the United States of America of several mutations giving the same visual colouration—that is, birds having the normal markings but with either yellow or white body colour. These have been named Clearbodies and judging from the information and skins seen of this form the name is very apt. They are in fact the opposite to the Clearwings and pose interesting experiments for genetical enthusiasts. The material I have seen of these Clearbodies shows that the markings are very intense and in the normal form quite black and standing out very sharply in contrast with the clear yellow or white body colour. It is hoped that in due course specimens of this form will be seen in this country both in the aviaries of breeders and later on the show benches.

There are several composite types which seem to have made quite an impact with some breeders and are known by separate names. The most prominent of these are the Yellow-faced Opaline Whitewings, or as they are more popularly known 'Rainbows'. This latter is a very good name as these birds show a very great range of different bright colourings. Their correct genetical name indicates that they are a combination of the Yellow-faced Blue, Opaline and Clearwing characters in one bird. It will of course be realized that as all these three characters operate in a different genetical manner it naturally can take several generations to produce birds carrying all three at the same time. However, at the present time breeders need not start from the basic colourings as there are numerous specimens available that carry a part combination and therefore the end result can be achieved much more quickly.

I will not enumerate all the many different combinations that can give varying percentages of 'Rainbows' as it would take up far too much space, but I will give a selection so that breeders can have some choice.

If a Yellow-faced White Blue (that is the Yellow-faced form of the ordinary White) hen is mated to an Opaline Cobalt/Whitewing cock a percentage of the young hens will be 'Rainbows'. An Opaline

Whitewing Cobalt cock paired to a Yellow-faced Blue/White will also give a percentage of 'Rainbow' hens. By pairing a Yellow-faced Cobalt/Opaline Whitewing cock to an Opaline White Blue hen both cocks and hens of the 'Rainbow' type will be produced. The pairing of Yellow-faced Opaline Whitewing ('Rainbow') to Opaline Whitewing will again give 'Rainbows' of both sexes. A normal Cobalt/ Opaline Whitewing cock paired with a normal Yellow-faced Blue/ White hen will also produce a small percentage of 'Rainbows' even though both the parents appear virtually as Normals. It will be seen from these specimen pairings that there are many other crosses which can be used in the production of 'Rainbows' in their various colour ranges. In the breeding of these birds the grey colouring should be avoided as the Yellow-faced Opaline White Greys, although technically 'Rainbows', are not very inspiring in their colour because of the masking character of Grey. The Cobalt and Violet forms of the 'Rainbows' give the best and most varied bright colour effect.

Another composite type which at one time was quite popular is the Full Body Coloured Greywings which have quite an interesting breeding behaviour in addition to their rather attractive colouration. These birds are the result of combining the Clearwing character with the Greywing character which gives birds quite different from either parent. As their name indicates, this form has grey wings and a body colouring which is more or less the same as that of ordinary Normals. When one of these Full Body Coloured Greywings is paired to a Normal White or a Normal Yellow then half the young are Clearwings and half Greywings—quite an interesting result. Now if one is paired to a Greywing then half the young are Greywing and half Full Body Coloured Greywings and the reverse pairing will give Clearwings and Full Body Coloured Greywings.

As both Clearwings and Greywings that are met with at the present time are mostly 'split' for Yellow or White the result of pairing them together produces a range of types. This fact has rather puzzled breeders as Normal Yellows, Whites, Clearwings and Greywings can appear in the same nests as the Full Body Coloured Greywings.

Some very interesting forms of these Full Body Coloured Greywings have been bred, particularly those which have combined the Violet and Opaline characters producing a very highly coloured combination. It will be seen that the production of the

Greywing Clearwing combination can be most exciting to the colour breeder and many unusual colour forms can be bred.

It is a long time since the Fallow varieties enjoyed real popularity with breeders, but during that time some rather strangely coloured specimens were evolved. A form of Red-eyed 'Clearbody' can be produced by combining the Fallow, Opaline and Grey characters in one bird. When these specimens are bred their body colour is more or less clear white or yellow and their markings are steely grey with the opaline pattern. It will be fairly obvious to breeders that the production of these rather fascinating birds must take several generations, particularly as the breeding material is very limited at the present time. The main thing to obtain at the present time is one of the Fallow kinds, either German or English, it does not matter which, and pair the bird to an Opaline Grey. From such a cross the young will be 'split' for Fallow and Opaline and will be either grey or normal in colour. If the Opaline Grey used happens to be a cock bird then of course all the hens will be Opalines in Grey or Normal and 'split' for Fallow. An Opaline Grey/Fallow hen paired to a Normal/Opaline Fallow cock will give a small percentage of the desired Opaline Fallow Greys. Once a few specimens have been obtained the breeder can then arrange his pairings so that both cocks and hens of this composite type can be produced in greater numbers.

When the Grey character is combined with the Violet character the resulting birds carrying both these characters are of a soft mauve tinted shade much warmer than the usual dull grey tone. The cheek flashes are very dark and dull but the two long central tail feathers remain black. Light, medium and dark Violet Greys all have the same warm tone of colour and can be had in all varieties including Grey Greens where the body shade is a darker and warmer tone.

Other colour forms which have been produced in this country are the English Grey, which is a darker form of the Australian Grey but of a Recessive manner of inheritance, and the Recessive Brown-wing which is similar to the Cinnamon in general colour. At the present time both of these forms seem to be practically non-existent but may of course reappear at any time as it is possible for such Recessive characters to be handed down for many generations and only reappear when suitable pairings are made.

At odd times Red, Pink and Black Budgerigars have been reported nothing but Light Greens will be pure-bred. The others, however, may be split for yellow or for white (lgr/w × ly also yields 50% outwardly similar Light Greens and 50% outwardly similar Yellows). The latter may be ly or ly/w birds, the former lgr/y or lgr/w birds. It follows that the sole use of such test matings lies in the possibility of selecting the pure-breds.

as having been produced, but I have not yet had the pleasure of seeing any of these birds. I feel that any specimens which could claim any resemblance to these colours owe them to unnatural causes, but nevertheless we may yet get a mutation to give us quite a surprise and we could see Red or Black Budgerigars in our aviaries.

Illustrations: Plates 60, 62–65.

APPENDIX

PERCENTAGE TABLES OF THE NORMAL COLOURS

Key to abbreviations and numbers and to the use of tables

lgr	Light Green	No. 1
dgr	Dark Green	No. 2
ogr	Olive Green	No. 3
ly	Light Yellow	No. 4
dy	Dark Yellow	No. 5
oy	Olive Yellow	No. 6
sb	Sky Blue	No. 7
cb	Cobalt	No. 8
ma	Mauve	No. 9
wsb	White Sky Blue	No. 10
wcb	White Cobalt	No. 11
wma	White Mauve	No. 12
lgr/y	Light Green/Yellow	No. 13
dgr/y	Dark Green/Yellow	No. 14
ogr/y	Olive Green/Yellow	No. 15
lgr/b	Light Green/Blue	No. 16
dgr/bI	Dark Green/Blue Type I	No. 17
dgr/bII	Dark Green/Blue Type II	No. 18
ogr/b	Olive Green/Blue	No. 19
lgr/w	Light Green/White	No. 20
dg/rwI	Dark Green/White Type I	No. 21
dgr/wII	Dark Green/White Type II	No. 22
ogr/w	Olive Green/White	No. 23
ly/w	Light Yellow/White	No. 24
dy/wI	Dark Yellow/White Type I	No. 25
dy/wII	Dark Yellow/White Type II	No. 26
oy/w	Olive Yellow/White	No. 27
sb/w	Sky Blue/White	No. 28
cb/w	Cobalt/White	No. 29
ma/w	Mauve/White	No. 30

Green is represented by the abbreviation gr. The abbreviation gw will serve to identify the Greywings, whereas the Greys may be conveniently abbreviated gy.

When a bird is split for a certain colour the fact is indicated by a bar / between the letters.

A few examples will serve to illustrate the use of the tables.

Suppose we want to cross a Sky Blue to a White Mauve. For these birds, we find the following abbreviations and numbers: sb = No. 7 and wma = No. 12. What we have to do is to look up, in table No. 7, combination 7 × 12, sb × wm. We shall then find the number 100 under No. 29, indicating the expectation percentage. The number 29 is cb/w, the expectation is 100% Cobalts split for white.

Another example:

We are crossing a Light Yellow to a Light Green split for blue. Light Yellow (ly) is No. 4, Light Green/Blue (lgr/b) is No. 16. Table 4, under 4 × 16, gives 50% under 13 and 50% under 20. Our expectation is an equal number of Light Greens split for yellow and Light Greens split for white.

Outwardly, these birds are all exactly alike, and when intending to cross them to each other we look up Table 13 under combination 13 × 20 finding 13% lgr, 13% ly, 25% lgr/y, 13% lgr/b, 25% lgr/w and 13% ogr/w. The Light Greens are exactly alike but will differ in the qualities they transmit. In breeding the Light Yellows and the Olive Greens will be the only chicks we are concerned with.

Using the tables will facilitate establishing the birds useful for breeding purposes. In a clutch containing chicks differing in outward appearance, i.e. in colour, and not split for any other colour, we are dealing with pure-breds.

If, on the other hand, the table gives three different kinds of Light Greens, as for instance lgr, lgr/y and lgr/w (vide Table 16 under 16 × 13) and ogr/y birds the latter are the only chicks we may be certain about. The Olive Greens will be split for yellow, that much we know. The Light Greens, though, are all alike, and test matings will be the only means of establishing which of them are pure-bred. A good cross for the purpose would be a cross to a pure-bred Light Yellow. Consulting Table 4, we shall find lgr × ly yields 100% lgr/y birds, all of them outwardly light-green. Lgr/y × ly, on the other hand, yields 50% ly and 50% lgr/y. The Light Greens producing nothing but Light Greens will be pure-bred. The others, however, may be split for yellow or for white (lgr/w × ly also yields 50% outwardly similar Light Greens and 50% outwardly similar Yellows). The latter may be ly or ly/w birds, the former lgr/y or lgr/w birds. It follows that the sole use of such test matings lies in the possibility of selecting the pure-breds.

COLOUR PERCENTAGE TABLE No. 1 LIGHT GREEN (LGR)

LGR = 1	1	2	3	4	5	6	7	8	9	10	11	12	13	14	15	16	17	18	19	20	21	22	23	24	25	26	27	28	29	30	
1 × 1 lgr	100																														1
1 × 2 dgr	50	50																													2
1 × 3 ogr		100																													3
1 × 4 ly													100																		4
1 × 5 dy													50	50																	5
1 × 6 oy														100																	6
1 × 7 sb																100															7
1 × 8 cb																50		50													8
1 × 9 ma																		100													9
1 × 10 wsb																				100											10
1 × 11 wcb																				50		50									11
1 × 12 wma																						100									12
1 × 13 lgr/y	50												50																		13
1 × 14 dgr/y	25	25											25	25																	14
1 × 15 ogr/y		50												50																	15
1 × 16 lgr/b	50															50															16
1 × 17 dgr/bI	8	42														42		8													17
1 × 18 dgr/bII	42	8														8		42													18
1 × 19 ogr/b		50																50													19
1 × 20 lgr/w	25												25			25				25											20
1 × 21 dgr/wI	4	21											4	21		21		4		21		4									21
1 × 22 dgr/wII	21	4											21	4		4		21		4		21									22
1 × 23 ogr/w		25												25				25				25									23
1 × 24 ly/w													50							50											24
1 × 25 dy/wI													8	42						42		8									25
1 × 26 dy/wII													42	8						8		42									26
1 × 27 oy/w														50								50									27
1 × 28 sb/w																50				50											28
1 × 29 cb/w																25		25		25		25									29
1 × 30 ma/w																		50				50									30
	1	2	3	4	5	6	7	8	9	10	11	12	13	14	15	16	17	18	19	20	21	22	23	24	25	26	27	28	29	30	

COLOUR PERCENTAGE TABLE No. 2 DARK GREEN (DGR)

DGR = 2	1	2	3	4	5	6	7	8	9	10	11	12	13	14	15	16	17	18	19	20	21	22	23	24	25	26	27	28	29.	30	
2 × 1 lgr	50	50																													1
2 × 2 dgr	25	50	25																												2
2 × 3 ogr		50	50																												3
2 × 4 ly													50	50																	4
2 × 5 dy													25	50	25																5
2 × 6 oy														50	50																6
2 × 7 sb																50	50														7
2 × 8 cb																25	25	25	25												8
2 × 9 ma																		50	50												9
2 × 10 wsb																				50	50										10
2 × 11 wcb																				25	25	25	25								11
2 × 12 wma																						50	50								12
2 × 13 lgr/y	25	25											25	25																	13
2 × 14 dgr/y	13	25	13										13	25	13																14
2 × 15 ogr/y		25	25											25	25																15
2 × 16 lgr/b	25	25														25	25														16
2 × 17 dgr/bI	4	25	21													21	21	4	4												17
2 × 18 dgr/bII	21	25	4													4	4	21	21												18
2 × 19 ogr/b		25	25															25	25												19
2 × 20 lgr/w	13	13											13	13		13	13			13	13										20
2 × 21 dgr/wI	2	13	11										2	13	11	11	11	2	2	11	11	2	2								21
2 × 22 dgr/wII	11	13	2										11	13	2	2	2	11	11	2	2	11	11								22
2 × 23 ogr/w		13	13											13	13			13	13			13	13								23
2 × 24 ly/w													25	25						25	25										24
2 × 25 dy/wI													4	25	21					21	21	4	4								25
2 × 26 dy/wII													21	25	4					4	4	21	21								26
2 × 27 oy/w														25	25							25	25								27
2 × 28 sb/w																25	25			25	25										28
2 × 29 cb/w																13	13	13	13	13	13	13	13								29
2 × 30 ma/w																		25	25			25	25								30
	1	2	3	4	5	6	7	8	9	10	11	12	13	14	15	16	17	18	19	20	21	22	23	24	25	26	27	28	29	30	

COLOUR PERCENTAGE TABLE No. 3 OLIVE GREEN (OGR)

OGR = 3	1	2	3	4	5	6	7	8	9	10	11	12	13	14	15	16	17	18	19	20	21	22	23	24	25	26	27	28	29	30	
3 × 1 lgr		100																													1
3 × 2 dgr		50	50																												2
3 × 3 ogr			100																												3
3 × 4 ly														100																	4
3 × 5 dy														50	50																5
3 × 6 oy															100																6
3 × 7 sb																	100														7
3 × 8 cb																	50		50												8
3 × 9 ma																			100												9
3 × 10 wsb																					100										10
3 × 11 wcb																					50		50								11
3 × 12 wma																							100								12
3 × 13 lgr/y		50												50																	13
3 × 14 dgr/y		25	25											25	25																14
3 × 15 ogr/y			50												50																15
3 × 16 lgr/b		50															50														16
3 × 17 dgr/bI		8	42														42		8												17
3 × 18 dgr/bII		42	8														8		42												18
3 × 19 ogr/b			50																50												19
3 × 20 lgr/w		25												25			25				25										20
3 × 21 dgr/wI		4	21										4		21		21		4		21		4								21
3 × 22 dgr/wII		21	4										21		4		4		21		4		21								22
3 × 23 ogr/w			25												25				25				25								23
3 × 24 ly/w														50							50										24
3 × 25 dy/wI														8	42						42		8								25
3 × 26 dy/wII														42	8						8		42								26
3 × 27 oy/w															50								50								27
3 × 28 sb/w																	50				50										28
3 × 29 cb/w																	25		25		25		25								29
3 × 30 ma/w																			50				50								30
	1	2	3	4	5	6	7	8	9	10	11	12	13	14	15	16	17	18	19	20	21	22	23	24	25	26	27	28	29	30	

COLOUR PERCENTAGE TABLE No. 4 LIGHT YELLOW (LY)

LY = 4

	1	2	3	4	5	6	7	8	9	10	11	12	13	14	15	16	17	18	19	20	21	22	23	24	25	26	27	28	29	30	
4 × 1 lgr													100																		1
4 × 2 dgr													50	50																	2
4 × 3 ogr														100																	3
4 × 4 ly				100																											4
4 × 5 dy				50	50																										5
4 × 6 oy					100																										6
4 × 7 sb																				100											7
4 × 8 cb																				50		50									8
4 × 9 ma																						100									9
4 × 10 wsb																								100							10
4 × 11 wcb																								50		50					11
4 × 12 wma																										100					12
4 × 13 lgr/y				50									50																		13
4 × 14 dgr/y				25	25								25	25																	14
4 × 15 ogr/y					50									50																	15
4 × 16 lgr/b													50							50											16
4 × 17 dgr/bI													8	42						42		8									17
4 × 18 dgr/bII													42	8						8		42									18
4 × 19 ogr/b														50								50									19
4 × 20 lgr/w				25									25							25				25							20
4 × 21 dgr/wI				4	21								4	21						21		4		21		4					21
4 × 22 dgr/wII				21	4								21	4						4		21		4		21					22
4 × 23 ogr/w					25									25								25				25					23
4 × 24 ly/w				50																				50							24
4 × 25 dy/wI				8	42																			42		8					25
4 × 26 dy/wII				42	8																			8		42					26
4 × 27 oy/w					50																					50					27
4 × 28 sb/w																				50				50							28
4 × 29 cb/w																				25		25		25		25					29
4 × 30 ma/w																						50				50					30
	1	2	3	4	5	6	7	8	9	10	11	12	13	14	15	16	17	18	19	20	21	22	23	24	25	26	27	28	29	30	

COLOUR PERCENTAGE TABLE No. 5 DARK YELLOW (DY)

DY = 5

	1	2	3	4	5	6	7	8	9	10	11	12	13	14	15	16	17	18	19	20	21	22	23	24	25	26	27	28	29	30	
5 × 1 lgr													50	50																	1
5 × 2 dgr													25	50	25																2
5 × 3 ogr														50	50																3
5 × 4 ly				50	50																										4
5 × 5 dy				25	50	25																									5
5 × 6 oy					50	50																									6
5 × 7 sb																				50	50										7
5 × 8 cb																				25	25	25	25								8
5 × 9 ma																						50	50								9
5 × 10 wsb																								50	50						10
5 × 11 wcb																								25	25	25	25				11
5 × 12 wma																										50	50				12
5 × 13 lgr/y				25	25								25	25																	13
5 × 14 dgr/y				13	25	13							13	25	13																14
5 × 15 ogr/y					25	25								25	25																15
5 × 16 lgr/b													25	25						25	25										16
5 × 17 dgr/bI													4	25	21					21	21	4	4								17
5 × 18 dgr/bII													21	25	4					4	4	21	21								18
5 × 19 ogr/b														25	25							25	25								19
5 × 20 lgr/w				13	13								13	13						13	13			13	13						20
5 × 21 dgr/wI				2	13	11							2	13	11					11	11	2	2	11	11	2	2				21
5 × 22 dgr/wII				11	13	2							11	13	2					2	2	11	11	2	2	11	11				22
5 × 23 ogr/w					13	13								13	13							13	13			13	13				23
5 × 24 ly/w				25	25																			25		25					24
5 × 25 dy/wI				4	25	21																		21	21	4	4				25
5 × 26 dy/wII				21	25	4																		4	4	21	21				26
5 × 27 oy/w					25	25																				25	25				27
5 × 28 sb/w																				25	25			25	25						28
5 × 29 cb/w																				13	13	13	13	13	13	13	13				29
5 × 30 ma/w																						25	25			25	25				30
	1	2	3	4	5	6	7	8	9	10	11	12	13	14	15	16	17	18	19	20	21	22	23	24	25	26	27	28	29	30	

COLOUR PERCENTAGE TABLE No. 6 OLIVE YELLOW (OY)

OY = 6	1	2	3	4	5	6	7	8	9	10	11	12	13	14	15	16	17	18	19	20	21	22	23	24	25	26	27	28	29	30	
6 × 1 lgr														100																	1
6 × 2 dgr														50	50																2
6 × 3 ogr															100																3
6 × 4 ly					100																										4
6 × 5 dy					50	50																									5
6 × 6 oy						100																									6
6 × 7 sb																					100										7
6 × 8 cb																					50		50								8
6 × 9 ma																							100								9
6 × 10 wsb																									100						10
6 × 11 wcb																									50		50				11
6 × 12 wma																											100				12
6 × 13 lgr/y					50									50																	13
6 × 14 dgr/y					25	25								25	25																14
6 × 15 ogr/y						50									50																15
6 × 16 lgr/b														50							50										16
6 × 17 dgr/bI														8	42						42		8								17
6 × 18 dgr/bII														42	8						8		42								18
6 × 19 ogr/b															50								50								19
6 × 20 lgr/w					25									25							25				25						20
6 × 21 dgr/wI					4	21								4	21						21		4		21		4				21
6 × 22 dgr/wII					21	4								21	4						4		21		4		21				22
6 × 23 ogr/w						25									25								25				25				13
6 × 24 ly/w					50																				50						24
6 × 25 dy/wI					8	42																			42		8				25
6 × 26 dy/wII					42	8																			42		8				26
6 × 27 oy/w						50																					50				27
6 × 28 sb/w																					50				50						28
6 × 29 cb/w																					25		25		25		25				29
6 × 30 ma/w																							50				50				30
	1	2	3	4	5	6	7	8	9	10	11	12	13	14	15	16	17	18	19	20	21	22	23	24	25	26	27	28	29	30	

COLOUR PERCENTAGE TABLE No. 7 SKY BLUE (SB)

SB = 7	1	2	3	4	5	6	7	8	9	10	11	12	13	14	15	16	17	18	19	20	21	22	23	24	25	26	27	28	29	30	
7 × 1 lgr																100															1
7 × 2 dgr																50	50														2
7 × 3 ogr																	100														3
7 × 4 ly																				100											4
7 × 5 dy																				50	50										5
7 × 6 oy																					100										6
7 × 7 sb							100																								7
7 × 8 cb							50	50																							8
7 × 9 ma								100																							9
7 × 10 wsb																												100			10
7 × 11 wcb																												50	50		11
7 × 12 wma																													100		12
7 × 13 lgr/y																50				50											13
7 × 14 dgr/y																25	25			25	25										14
7 × 15 ogr/y																	50				50										15
7 × 16 lgr/b							50									50															16
7 × 17 dgr/bI							42	8								8	42														17
7 × 18 dgr/bII							8	42								42	8														18
7 × 19 ogr/b								50									50														19
7 × 20 lgr/w							25									25				25								25			20
7 × 21 dgr/wI							21	4								4	21			4	21							21	4		21
7 × 22 dgr/wII							4	21								21	4			21	4							4	21		22
7 × 23 ogr/w								25									25				25								25		23
7 × 24 ly/w																				50								50			24
7 × 25 dy/wI																				8	42							42	8		25
7 × 26 dy/wII																				42	8							8	42		26
7 × 27 oy/w																					50								50		27
7 × 28 sb/w							50																					50			28
7 × 29 cb/w							25	25																				25	25		29
7 × 30 ma/w								50																					50		30
	1	2	3	4	5	6	7	8	9	10	11	12	13	14	15	16	17	18	19	20	21	22	23	24	25	26	27	28	29	30	

COLOUR PERCENTAGE TABLE No. 8 COBALT (CB)

CB = 8	1	2	3	4	5	6	7	8	9	10	11	12	13	14	15	16	17	18	19	20	21	22	23	24	25	26	27	28	29	30	
8 × 1 lgr																50		50													1
8 × 2 dgr																25	25	25	25												2
8 × 3 ogr																	50		50												3
8 × 4 ly																				50		50									4
8 × 5 dy																				25	25	25	25								5
8 × 6 oy																					50		50								6
8 × 7 sb							50	50																							7
8 × 8 cb							25	50	25																						8
8 × 9 ma								50	50																						9
8 × 10 wsb																												50	50		10
8 × 11 wcb																												25	50	25	11
8 × 12 wma																													50	50	12
8 × 13 lgr/y																25		25		25		25									13
8 × 14 dgr/y																13	13	13	13	13	13	13	13								14
8 × 15 ogr/y																	25		25		25		25								15
8 × 16 lgr/b							25	25								25		25													16
8 × 17 dgr/bI							21	25	4							4	21	4	21												17
8 × 18 dgr/bII							4	25	21							21	4	21	4												18
8 × 19 ogr/b								25	25								25		25												19
8 × 20 lgr/w							13	13								13		13		13		13					13	13			20
8 × 21 dgr/wI							11	13	2							2	11	2	11	2	11	2	11					11	13	2	21
8 × 22 dgr/wII								2	13	11						11	2	11	2	11	2	11	2					2	13	11	22
8 × 23 ogr/w								13	13								13		13		13		13						13	13	23
8 × 24 ly/w																				25		25						25	25		24
8 × 25 dy/wI																				4	21	4	21					21	25	4	25
8 × 26 dy/wII																				21	4	21	4					4	25	21	26
8 × 27 oy/w																					25		25						25	25	27
8 × 28 sb/w							25	25																				25	25		28
8 × 29 cb/w							13	25	13																			13	25	13	29
8 × 30 ma/w								25	25																				25	25	30
	1	2	3	4	5	6	7	8	9	10	11	12	13	14	15	16	17	18	19	20	21	22	23	24	25	26	27	28	29	30	

COLOUR PERCENTAGE TABLE No. 9 MAUVE (MA)

MA = 9	1	2	3	4	5	6	7	8	9	10	11	12	13	14	15	16	17	18	19	20	21	22	23	24	25	26	27	28	29	30	
9 × 1 lgr																		100													1
9 × 2 dgr																		50	50												2
9 × 3 ogr																			100												3
9 × 4 ly																						100									4
9 × 5 dy																						50	50								5
9 × 6 oy																							100								6
9 × 7 sb								100																							7
9 × 8 cb								50	50																						8
9 × 9 ma									100																						9
9 × 10 wsb																													100		10
9 × 11 wcb																													50	50	11
9 × 12 wma																														100	12
9 × 13 lgr/y																		50				50									13
9 × 14 dgr/y																		25	25			25	25								14
9 × 15 ogr/y																			50				50								15
9 × 16 lgr/b								50										50													16
9 × 17 dgr/bI								42	8									8	42												17
9 × 18 dgr/bII								8	42									42	8												18
9 × 19 ogr/b									50										50												19
9 × 20 lgr/w								25										25				25							25		20
9 × 21 dgr/wI								21	4									4	21			4	21						21	4	21
9 × 22 dgr/wII								4	21									21	4			21	4						4	21	22
9 × 23 ogr/w									25										25			25								25	23
9 × 24 ly/w																						50							50		24
9 × 25 dy/wI																						8	42						42	8	25
9 × 26 dy/wII																						42	8						8	42	26
9 × 27 oy/w																							50							50	27
9 × 28 sb/w								50																					50		28
9 × 29 cb/w								25	25																				25	25	29
9 × 30 ma/w									50																					20	30
	1	2	3	4	5	6	7	8	9	10	11	12	13	14	15	16	17	18	19	20	21	22	23	24	25	26	27	28	29	30	

COLOUR PERCENTAGE TABLE No. 10 WHITE SKY BLUE (WSB)

WSB = 10	1	2	3	4	5	6	7	8	9	10	11	12	13	14	15	16	17	18	19	20	21	22	23	24	25	26	27	28	29	30	
10 × 1 lgr																				100											1
10 × 2 dgr																				50	50										2
10 × 3 ogr																					100										3
10 × 4 ly																								100							4
10 × 5 dy																								50	50						5
10 × 6 oy																									100						6
10 × 7 sb																												100			7
10 × 8 cb																												50	50		8
10 × 9 ma																													100		9
10 × 10 wsb										100																					10
10 × 11 wcb										50	50																				11
10 × 12 wma											100																				12
10 × 13 lgr/y																				50				50							13
10 × 14 dgr/y																				25	25			25	25						14
10 × 15 ogr/y																					50				50						15
10 × 16 lgr/b																				50								50			16
10 × 17 dgr/bI																				8	42							42	8		17
10 × 18 dgr/bII																				42	8							8	42		18
10 × 19 ogr/b																					50								50		19
10 × 20 lgr/w										25										25				25				25			20
10 × 21 dgr/wI										21	4									4	21			4	21			21	4		21
10 × 22 dgr/wII										4	21									21	4			21	4			4	21		22
10 × 23 ogr/w											25										25				25				25		23
10 × 24 ly/w										50														50							24
10 × 25 dy/wI										42	8													8	42						25
10 × 26 dy/wII										8	42													42	8						26
10 × 27 oy/w											50														50						27
10 × 28 sb/w										50																		50			28
10 × 29 cb/w										25	25																	25	25		29
10 × 30 ma/w											50																		50		30
	1	2	3	4	5	6	7	8	9	10	11	12	13	14	15	16	17	18	19	20	21	22	23	24	25	26	27	28	29	30	

COLOUR PERCENTAGE TABLE No. 11 WHITE COBALT (WCB)

WCB = 11	1	2	3	4	5	6	7	8	9	10	11	12	13	14	15	16	17	18	19	20	21	22	23	24	25	26	27	28	29	30	
11 × 1 lgr																				50		50									1
11 × 2 dgr																				25	25	25	25								2
11 × 3 ogr																					50		50								3
11 × 4 ly																								50		50					4
11 × 5 dy																								25	25	25	25				5
11 × 6 oy																									50		50				6
11 × 7 sb																												50	50		7
11 × 8 cb																												25	50	25	8
11 × 9 ma																													50	50	9
11 × 10 wsb										50	50																				10
11 × 11 wcb										25	50	25																			11
11 × 12 wma											50	50																			12
11 × 13 lgr/y																				25		25		25		25					13
11 × 14 dgr/y																				13	13	13	13	13	13	13	13				14
11 × 15 ogr/y																					25		25		25		25				15
11 × 16 lgr/b																				25		25						25	25		16
11 × 17 dgr/bI																				4	21	4	21					21	25	4	17
11 × 18 dgr/bII																				21	4	21	4					4	25	21	18
11 × 19 ogr/b																					25		25						25	25	19
11 × 20 lgr/w										13	13									13		13		13		13		13	13		20
11 × 21 dgr/wI										11	13	2								2	11	2	11	2	11	2	11	11	13	2	21
11 × 22 dgr/wII										2	13	11								11	2	11	2	11	2	11	2	2	13	11	22
11 × 23 ogr/w											13	13									13		13		13		13		13	13	23
11 × 24 ly/w										25	25													25		25					24
11 × 25 dy/wI										21	25	4												4	21	4	21				25
11 × 26 dy/wII										4	25	21												21	4	21	4				26
11 × 27 oy/w											25	25													25		25				27
11 × 28 sb/w										25	25																	25	25		28
11 × 29 cb/w										13	13	13																13	25	13	29
11 × 30 ma/w											25	25																	25	25	30
	1	2	3	4	5	6	7	8	9	10	11	12	13	14	15	16	17	18	19	20	21	22	23	24	25	26	27	28	29	30	

WMA = 12

	1	2	3	4	5	6	7	8	9	10	11	12	13	14	15	16	17	18	19	20	21	22	23	24	25	26	27	28	29	30	
12 × 1 lgr																						100									1
12 × 2 dgr																						50	50								2
12 × 3 ogr																							100								3
12 × 4 ly																										100					4
12 × 5 dy																										50	50				5
12 × 6 oy																											100				6
12 × 7 sb																													100		7
12 × 8 cb																													50	50	8
12 × 9 ma																														100	9
12 × 10 wsb											100																				10
12 × 11 wcb											50	50																			11
12 × 12 wma												100																			12
12 × 13 lgr/y																						50				50					13
12 × 14 dgr/y																						25	25			25	25				14
12 × 15 ogr/y																							50				50				15
12 × 16 lgr/b																						50							50		16
12 × 17 dgr/bI																						8	42						42	8	17
12 × 18 dgr/bII																						42	8						42	8	18
12 × 19 ogr/b																							50							50	19
12 × 20 lgr/w											25											25				25			25		20
12 × 21 dgr/wI											21	4										4	21			4	21		21	4	21
12 × 22 dgr/wII											4	21										21	4			21	4		4	21	22
12 × 23 ogr/w												25											25				25			25	23
12 × 24 ly/w											50															50					24
12 × 25 dy/wI											42	8														8	42				25
12 × 26 dy/wII											8	42														42	8				26
12 × 27 oy/w												50															50				27
12 × 28 sb/w											50																		50		28
12 × 29 cb/w											25	25																	25	25	29
12 × 30 ma/w												50																		50	30
	1	2	3	4	5	6	7	8	9	10	11	12	13	14	15	16	17	18	19	20	21	22	23	24	25	26	27	28	29	30	

COLOUR PERCENTAGE TABLE No. 13 LIGHT GREEN / YELLOW (LGR/Y)

LGR/Y = 13	1	2	3	4	5	6	7	8	9	10	11	12	13	14	15	16	17	18	19	20	21	22	23	24	25	26	27	28	29	30	
13 × 1 lgr	50												50																		1
13 × 2 dgr	25	25											25	25																	2
13 × 3 ogr		50												50																	3
13 × 4 ly				50									50																		4
13 × 5 dy				25	25								25	25																	5
13 × 6 oy					50									50																	6
13 × 7 sb																50				50											7
13 × 8 cb																25		25		25		25									8
13 × 9 ma																		50				50									9
13 × 10 wsb																				50				50							10
13 × 11 wcb																				25		25		25		25					11
13 × 12 wma																						50				50					12
13 × 13 lgr/y	25			25									50																		13
13 × 14 dgr/y	13	13		13	13								25	25																	14
13 × 15 ogr/y		25			25									50																	15
13 × 16 lgr/b	25												25			25				25											16
13 × 17 dgr/bI	4	21											4	21		21		4		21		4									17
13 × 18 dgr/bII	21	4											21	4		4		21		4		21									18
13 × 19 ogr/b		25												25				25				25									19
13 × 20 lgr/w	13			13									25			13				25				13							20
13 × 21 dgr/wI	2	11		2	11								4	21		11		2		21		4		11		2					21
13 × 22 dgr/wII	11	2		11	2								4	21		2		11		21		4		2		11					22
13 × 23 ogr/w		13			13									25				13				25				13					23
13 × 24 ly/w				25									25							25				25							24
13 × 25 dy/wI				4	21								4	21						21		4		21		4					25
13 × 26 dy/wII				21	4								21	4						4		21		4		21					26
13 × 27 oy/w					25									25								25				25					27
13 × 28 sb/w																25				50				25							28
13 × 29 cb/w																13		13		25		25		13		13					29
13 × 30 ma/w																		25				50				25					30

DGR/Y = 14	1	2	3	4	5	6	7	8	9	10	11	12	13	14	15	16	17	18	19	20	21	22	23	24	25	26	27	28	29	30	
14 × 1 lgr	25	25											25	25																	1
14 × 2 dgr	13	25	13										13	25	13																2
14 × 3 ogr		25	25											25	25																3
14 × 4 ly				25	25								25	25																	4
14 × 5 dy				13	25	13							13	25	13																5
14 × 6 oy					25	25								25	25																6
14 × 7 sb																25	25			25	25										7
14 × 8 cb																13	13	13	13	13	13	13	13								8
14 × 9 ma																		25	25				25			25					9
14 × 10 wsb																				25	25			25	25						10
14 × 11 wcb																				13	13	13	13	13	13	13	13				11
14 × 12 wma																						25	25			25	25				12
14 × 13 lgr/y	13	13		13	13								25	25																	13
14 × 14 dgr/y	6	13	6	6	13	6							13	25	13																14
14 × 15 ogr/y		13	13		13	13								25	25																15
14 × 16 lgr/b	13	13											13	13		13	13			13	13										16
14 × 17 dgr/bI	2	13	11										2	13	11	11	11	2	2	11	11	2	2								17
14 × 18 dgr/bII	11	13	2										11	13	2	2	2	11	11	2	2	11	11								18
14 × 19 ogr/b		13	13											13	13			13	13			13	13								19
14 × 20 lgr/w	6	6		6	6								13	13		6	6			13	13			6	6						20
14 × 21 dgr/wI	1	6	5	1	6	5							2	13	11	5	5	1	1	11	11	2	2	5	5	1	1				21
14 × 22 dgr/wII	5	6	1	5	6	1							11	13	2	1	1	5	5	2	2	11	11	1	1	5	5				22
14 × 23 ogr/w		6	6		6	6								13	13			6	6			13	13			6	6				23
14 × 24 ly/w				13	13								13	13						13	13			13	13						24
14 × 25 dy/wI				2	13	11							2	13	11					11	11	2	2	11	11	2	2				25
14 × 26 dy/wII				11	13	2							11	13	2					2	2	11	11	2	2	11	11				26
14 × 27 oy/w					13	13								13	13							13	13			13	13				27
14 × 28 sb/w																13	13			25	25			13	13						28
14 × 29 cb/w																6	6	6	6	13	13	13	13	6	6	6	6				29
14 × 30 ma/w																		13	13			25	25			13	13				30
	1	2	3	4	5	6	7	8	9	10	11	12	13	14	15	16	17	18	19	20	21	22	23	24	25	26	27	28	29	30	

COLOUR PERCENTAGE TABLE No. 15 OLIVE GREEN / YELLOW (OGR/Y)

OGR/Y = 15	1	2	3	4	5	6	7	8	9	10	11	12	13	14	15	16	17	18	19	20	21	22	23	24	25	26	27	28	29	30	
15 × 1 lgr		50												50																	1
15 × 2 dgr		25	25											25	25																2
15 × 3 ogr			50												50																3
15 × 4 ly					50									50																	4
15 × 5 dy					25	25								25	25																5
15 × 6 oy						50									50																6
15 × 7 sb																	50				50										7
15 × 8 cb																	25		25		25		25								8
15 × 9 ma																			50				50								9
15 × 10 wsb																					50				50						10
15 × 11 wcb																					25		25		25		25				11
15 × 12 wma																							50				50				12
15 × 13 lgr/y		25			25									50																	13
15 × 14 dgr/y		13	13		13	13								25	25																14
15 × 15 ogr/y			25			25									50																15
15 × 16 lgr/b		25												25			25				25										16
15 × 17 dgr/bI		4	21											4	21		21		4		21		4								17
15 × 18 dgr/bII		21	4											21	4		4		21		4		21								18
15 × 19 ogr/b			25												25				25				25								19
15 × 20 lgr/w		13			13									25			13				25				13						20
15 × 21 dgr/wI		2	11		2	11								4	21		11		2		21		4		11		2				21
15 × 22 dgr/wII		11	2		11	2								21	4		2		11		4		21		2		11				22
15 × 23 ogr/w			13			13									25				13				25				13				23
15 × 24 ly/w					25									25							25				25						24
15 × 25 dy/wI					4	21								4	21						21		4		21		4				25
15 × 26 dy/wII					21	4								21	4						4		21		4		21				26
15 × 27 oy/w						25									25								25				25				27
15 × 28 sb/w																	25				50				25						28
15 × 29 cb/w																	13		13		25		25		13		13				29
15 × 30 ma/w																			25				50				25				30
	1	2	3	4	5	6	7	8	9	10	11	12	13	14	15	16	17	18	19	20	21	22	23	24	25	26	27	28	29	30	

COLOUR PERCENTAGE TABLE No. 16 LIGHT GREEN / BLUE (LGR/B)

LGR/B = 16	1	2	3	4	5	6	7	8	9	10	11	12	13	14	15	16	17	18	19	20	21	22	23	24	25	26	27	28	29	30	
16 × 1 lgr	50															50															1
16 × 2 dgr	25	25														25	25														2
16 × 3 ogr		50															50														3
16 × 4 ly												50								50											4
16 × 5 dy												25	25							25	25										5
16 × 6 oy													50								50										6
16 × 7 sb							50									50															7
16 × 8 cb							25	25								25		25													8
16 × 9 ma								50										50													9
16 × 10 wsb																				50								50			10
16 × 11 wcb																				25		25						25	25		11
16 × 12 wma																						50							50		12
16 × 13 lgr/y	25												25			25				25											13
16 × 14 dgr/y	13	13											13	13		13	13			13	13										14
16 × 15 ogr/y		25												25			25				25										15
16 × 16 lgr/b	25						25									50															16
16 × 17 dgr/bI	4	21					21	4								25	21	4													17
16 × 18 dgr/bII	21	4					4	21								25	4	21													18
16 × 19 ogr/b		25						25									25	25													19
16 × 20 lgr/w	13						13						13			25				25								13			20
16 × 21 dgr/wI	2	11					11	2					2	11		13	11	2		13	11	2						11	2		21
16 × 22 dgr/wII	11	2					2	11					11	2		13	2	11		13	2	11						2	11		22
16 × 23 ogr/w		13						13						13			13	13			13	13							13		23
16 × 24 ly/w													25							50								25			24
16 × 25 dy/wI													4	21						25	21	4						21	4		25
16 × 26 dy/wII													21	4						25	4	21						4	21		26
16 × 27 oy/w														25							25	25							25		27
16 × 28 sb/w							25									25				25								25			28
16 × 29 cb/w							13	13								13		13		13		13						13	13		29
16 × 30 ma/w								25										25				25							25		30
	1	2	3	4	5	6	7	8	9	10	11	12	13	14	15	16	17	18	19	20	21	22	23	24	25	26	27	28	29	30	

COLOUR PERCENTAGE TABLE No. 17 DARK GREEN / BLUE TYPE I (DGR/BI)

DGR/BI = 17	1	2	3	4	5	6	7	8	9	10	11	12	13	14	15	16	17	18	19	20	21	22	23	24	25	26	27	28	29	30	
17 × 1 lgr	8	42														42		8													1
17 × 2 dgr	4	25	21													21	21	4	4												2
17 × 3 ogr		8	42														42		8												3
17 × 4 ly													8	42						42		8									4
17 × 5 dy													4	25	21					21	21	4	4								5
17 × 6 oy														8	42						42		8								6
17 × 7 sb							42	8								8	42														7
17 × 8 cb							21	25	4							4	21	4	21												8
17 × 9 ma								42	8									8	42												9
17 × 10 wsb																			8	42								42	8		10
17 × 11 wcb																				4	21	4	21					21	25	4	11
17 × 12 wma																						8	42						42	8	12
17 × 13 lgr/y	4	21											4	21		21		4		21		4									13
17 × 14 dgr/y	2	13	11										2	13	11	11	11	2	2	11	11	2	2								14
17 × 15 ogr/y		4	21											4	21		21		4		21		4								15
17 × 16 lgr/b	4	21					21	4								25	21	4													16
17 × 17 dgr/bI	2	4	18				18	4	2							4	36	4	4												17
17 × 18 dgr/bII	2	21	2				2	21	2							21	4	4	21												18
17 × 19 ogr/b		4	21					21	4								21	4	25												19
17 × 20 lgr/w	2	11					11	2					2	11		13	11	2		13	11	2						11	2		20
17 × 21 dgr/wI	1	11	1				1	11	1				1	11	1	2	11	2	10	10	2	11	2					1	11	1	21
17 × 22 dgr/wII	1	11	1				1	11	1				1	11	1	11	2	2	10	10	2	2	11					1	11	1	22
17 × 23 ogr/w		2	11					11	2					2	11		11	2	13		11	2	13						11	2	23
17 × 24 ly/w													4	21						25	21	4						21	4		24
17 × 25 dy/wI													2	13	11					13	21	4	13					11	13	2	25
17 × 26 dy/wII													11	13	2					13	4	21	13					2	13	11	26
17 × 27 oy/w														4	21						21	4	25						21	4	27
17 × 28 sb/w							21	4								4	21			4	21							21	4		28
17 × 29 cb/w							11	13	2							2	11	2	11	2	11	2	11					11	13	2	29
17 × 30 ma/w								21	4									4	21			4	21						21	4	30
	1	2	3	4	5	6	7	8	9	10	11	12	13	14	15	16	17	18	19	20	21	22	23	24	25	26	27	28	29	30	

COLOUR PERCENTAGE TABLE No. 18 DARK GREEN / BLUE TYPE II (DGR/BII)

DGR/BII = 18	1	2	3	4	5	6	7	8	9	10	11	12	13	14	15	16	17	18	19	20	21	22	23	24	25	6	27	28	29	30	
18 × 1 lgr	42	8														8		42													1
18 × 2 dgr	21	25	4													4	4	21	21												2
18 × 3 ogr		42	8														8		42												3
18 × 4 ly													42	8						8		42									4
18 × 5 dy													21	25	4					4	4	21	21								5
18 × 6 oy														42	8						8		42								6
18 × 7 sb							8	42								42	8														7
18 × 8 cb							4	25	21							21	4	21	4												8
18 × 9 ma								8	42									42	8												9
18 × 10 wsb																			42	8								8	42		10
18 × 11 wcb																				21	4	21	4					4	25	21	11
18 × 12 wma																						42	8						42	8	12
18 × 13 lgr/y	21	4											21	4		4		21		4		21									13
18 × 14 dgr/y	11	13	2										11	13	2	2	2	11	11	2	2	11	11								14
18 × 15 ogr/y		21	4											21	4		4		21		4		21								15
18 × 16 lgr/b	21	4					4	21								25	4	21													16
18 × 17 dgr/bI	2	21	2				2	21	2							21	4	4	21												17
18 × 18 dgr/bII	18	4	2				2	4	18							4	4	36	4												18
18 × 19 ogr/b		21	4					4	21								4	21	25												19
18 × 20 lgr/w	11	2					2	11					11	2		13	2	11		13	2	11						2	11		20
18 × 21 dgr/wI	1	11	1				1	11	1				1	11	1	2	2	21	2	2	21	2	2					1	11	1	21
18 × 22 dgr/wII	11	1	1				1	1	11				11	1	1	2	2	21	2	2	2	21	2					1	1	11	22
18 × 23 ogr/w		11	2					2	11					11	2		2	11	13		2	11	13						2	11	23
18 × 24 ly/w													21	4						25	4	21						4	21		24
18 × 25 dy/wI													11	13	2					13	4	21	13					2	13	11	25
18 × 26 dy/wII													2	13	11					13	4	21	13					2	13	11	26
18 × 27 oy/w														21	4						4	21	25						4	21	27
18 × 28 sb/w							21	4								4	21			4	21							21	4		28
18 × 29 cb/w							2	13	11							11	2	11	2	11	2	11	2					2	13	11	29
18 × 30 ma/w								4	21									21	4			21	4						4	11	30
	1	2	3	4	5	6	7	8	9	10	11	12	13	14	15	16	17	18	19	20	21	22	23	24	25	26	27	28	29	30	

COLOUR PERCENTAGE TABLE No. 19 OLIVE GREEN / BLUE (OGR/B)

OGR/B = 19	1	2	3	4	5	6	7	8	9	10	11	12	13	14	15	16	17	18	19	20	21	22	23	24	25	26	27	28	29	30	
19 × 1 lgr		50																50													1
19 × 2 dgr		25	25															25	25												2
19 × 3 ogr			50																50												3
19 × 4 ly														50								50									4
19 × 5 dy														25	25							25	25								5
19 × 6 oy															50								50								6
19 × 7 sb								50									50														7
19 × 8 cb								25	25								25		25												8
19 × 9 ma									50										50												9
19 × 10 wsb																					50								50		10
19 × 11 wcb																					25		25						25	25	11
19 × 12 wma																							50							50	12
19 × 13 lgr/y		25												25				25				25									13
19 × 14 dgr/y		13	13											13	13			13	13			13	13								14
19 × 15 ogr/y			25												25				25				25								15
19 × 16 lgr/b		25						25									25	25													16
19 × 17 dgr/bI		4	21					21	4								21	4	25												17
19 × 18 dgr/bII		21	4					4	21								4	21	25												18
19 × 19 ogr/b			25						25										50												19
19 × 20 lgr/w		13						13						13			13	13			13	13							13		20
19 × 21 dgr/wI		2	11					11	2					2	11		11	2	13		11	2	13						11	2	21
19 × 22 dgr/wII		11	2					2	11					11	2		2	11	13		2	11	13						2	11	22
19 × 23 ogr/w			13						13						13				25				25							13	23
19 ×.24 ly/w														25							25	25							25		24
19 × 25 dy/wI														4	21						21	4	25						21	4	25
19 × 26 dy/wII														21	4						4	21	25						4	21	26
19 × 27 oy/w															25								50							25	27
19 × 28 sb/w								25									25				25								25		28
19 × 29 cb/w								13	13								13		13		13		13						13	13	29
19 × 30 ma/w									25										25				25							25	30
	1	2	3	4	5	6	7	8	9	10	11	12	13	14	15	16	17	18	19	20	21	22	23	24	25	26	27	28	29	30	

COLOUR PERCENTAGE TABLE No. 20 LIGHT GREEN / WHITE (LGR/W)

LGR/W = 20	1	2	3	4	5	6	7	8	9	10	11	12	13	14	15	16	17	18	19	20	21	22	23	24	25	26	27	28	29	30	
20 × 1 lgr	25												25			25				25											1
20 × 2 dgr	13	13											13	13		13	13			13	13										2
20 × 3 ogr		25												25			25				25										3
20 × 4 ly				25									25							25				25							4
20 × 5 dy				13	13								13	13						13	13			13	13						5
20 × 6 oy					25									25							25				25						6
20 × 7 sb							25									25				25								25			7
20 × 8 cb							13	13								13		13		13		13						13	13		8
20 × 9 ma								25										25				25							25		9
20 × 10 wsb										25										25				25				25			10
20 × 11 wcb										13	13									13		13		13		13		13	13		11
20 × 12 wma											25											25				25			25		12
20 × 13 lgr/y	13			13									25			13				25			13								13
20 × 14 dgr/y	6	6		6	6								13	13		6	6			13	13		6	6							14
20 × 15 ogr/y		13			13									25			13				25			13							15
20 × 16 lgr/b	13						13						13			25				25								13			16
20 × 17 dgr/bI	2	11					11	2					2	11		13	11	2		13	11	2						11	2		17
20 × 18 dgr/bII	11	2					2	11					11	2		13	2	11		13	2	11						2	11		18
20 × 19 ogr/b		13						13						13			13	13			13	13							13		19
20 × 20 lgr/w	6			6			6			6			13			13				25				13				13			20
20 × 21 dgr/wI	1	5		1	5		5	1		5	1		2	11		6	5	1		13	11	2		6	5	1		11	2		21
20 × 22 dgr/wII	5	1		5	1		1	5		1	5		11	2		6	1	5		13	2	11		6	1	5		2	11		22
20 × 23 ogr/w		6			6			6			6			13			6	6			13	13			6	6			13		23
20 × 24 ly/w				13						13			13							25				25				13			24
20 × 25 dy/wI				2	11					11	2		2	11						13	11	2		13	11	2		11	2		25
20 × 26 dy/wII				11	2					2	11		11	2						13	2	11		13	2	11		2	11		26
20 × 27 oy/w					13						13			13							13	13			13	13			13		27
20 × 28 sb/w							13			13						3				25				13				25			28
20 × 29 cb/w							6	6		6	6					6		6		13		13		6		6		13	13		29
20 × 30 ma/w								13			13							13				25				13			25		30
	1	2	3	4	5	7	7	8	9	10	11	12	13	14	15	16	17	18	19	20	21	22	23	24	25	26	27	28	29	30	

COLOUR PERCENTAGE TABLE No. 21 DARK GREEN / WHITE TYPE I (DGR/WI)

DGR/WI = 21	1	2	3	4	5	6	7	8	9	10	11	12	13	14	15	16	17	18	19	20	21	22	23	24	25	26	27	28	29	30	
21 × 1 lgr	4	21											4	21		21		4		21		4									1
21 × 2 dgr	2	13	11										2	13	11	11	11	2	2	11	11	2	2								2
21 × 3 ogr		4	21											4	21		21		4		21		4								3
21 × 4 ly				4	21								4	21						21		4		21		4					4
21 × 5 dy				2	13	11							2	13	11					11	11	2	2	11	11	2	2				5
21 × 6 oy					4	21								4	21						21		4		21		4				6
21 × 7 sb							21	4								4	21			4	21							21	4		7
21 × 8 cb							11	13	2							2	11	2	11.	2	11	2	11					11	13	2	8
21 × 9 ma								21	4									4	21			4	21						21	4	9
21 × 10 wsb										21	4									4	21			4	21			21	4		10
21 × 11 wcb										11	13	2								2	11	2	11	2	11	2	11	11	13	2	11
21 × 12 wma											21	4										4	21			4	21		21	4	12
21 × 13 lgr/y	2	11		2	11								4	21		11		2		21		4		11		2					13
21 × 14 dgr/y	1	6	5	1	6	5							2	13	11	5	5	1	1	11	11	1	2	5	5	2	1				14
21 × 15 ogr/y		2	11		2	11								4	21		11		2		21		4		11		2				15
21 × 16 lgr/b	2	11					11	2					2	11		13	11	2		13	11	2						11	2		16
21 × 17 dgr/bI	1	11	1				1	11	1				1	11	1	2	11	2	10	10	2	11	2					1	11	1	17
21 × 18 dgr/bII	1	11	1				1	11	1				1	11	1	1	2	20	2	2	20	2	1					1	11	1	18
21 × 19 ogr/b		2	11					11	2					2	11		11	2	13		11	2	13						11	2	19
21 × 20 lgr/w	1	5		1	5		5	1		5	1		2	11		6	8	2		13	11	2		6	5	1		11	2		20
21 × 21 dgr/wI	1	2	3	1	2	3	3	2	1	3	2	1	2	4	8	2	8	2	2	4	10	4	4	2	8	2	2	8	4	2	21
21 × 22 dgr/wII	1	4	1	1	4	1	1	4	1	1	4	1	2	10	2	4	2	2	4	10	4	4	10	4	2	2	4	2	10	2	22
21 × 23 ogr/w		1	5		1	5		5	1		5	1		2	11		5	1	6		11	2	13		5	1	6		11	2	23
21 × 24 ly/w				2	11					11	2		2	11						13	11	2		13	11	2		11	2		24
21 × 25 dy/wI				1	10	2				2	10	1	1	10	2					2	20	2	2	2	20	2	2	2	10	1	25
21 × 26 dy/wII				2	10	1				1	10	2	2	10	1					10	2	2	10	10	2	2	10	1	10	2	26
21 × 27 oy/w					2	11					11	2		2	11						11	2	13		11	2	13		11	2	27
21 × 28 sb/w							11	2		11	2					2	11			4	21			2	11			21	4		28
21 × 29 cb/w							5	6	1	5	6	1				1	5	1	5	2	11	2	11	1	5	1	5	11	13	2	29
21 × 30 ma/w								11	2		11	2						2	11			4	21			2	11		21	4	30
	1	2	3	4	5	6	7	8	9	10	11	12	13	14	15	16	17	18	19	20	21	22	23	24	25	26	27	28	29	30	

COLOUR PERCENTAGE TABLE No. 22 DARK GREEN / WHITE TYPE II (DGR/WII)

DGR/WII = 22	1	2	3	4	5	6	7	8	9	10	11	12	13	14	15	16	17	18	19	20	21	22	23	24	25	26	27	28	29	30	
22 × 1 lgr	21	4											21	4		4		21		4		21									1
22 × 2 dgr	11	13	2										11	13	2	2	2	11	11	2	2	11	11								2
22 × 3 ogr		21	4											21	4		4		21		4		21								3
22 × 4 ly				21	4								21	4						4		21		4		21					4
22 × 5 dy				11	13	2							11	13	2					2	2	11	11	2	2	11	11				5
22 × 6 oy					21	4								21	4						4		21		4		21				6
22 × 7 sb							4	21								21	4			21	4							4	21		7
22 × 8 cb							2	13	11							11	2	11	2	11	2	11	2					2	13	11	8
22 × 9 ma								4	21									21	4			21	4						4	21	9
22 × 10 wsb										4	21									21	4			21	4			4	21		10
22 × 11 wcb										2	13	11								11	2	11	2	11	2	11	2	2	13	11	11
22 × 12 wma											4	21										21	4			21	4		4	21	12
22 × 13 lgr/y	11	2		11	2								4	21		2		11		21		4		2		11					13
22 × 14 dgr/y	5	6	1	5	6	1							11	13	2	1	1	5	5	2	2	11	11	1	1	5	5				14
22 × 15 ogr/y		11	2		11	2								21	4		2		11		4		21		2		11				15
22 × 16 lgr/b	11	2					2	11					11	2		13	2	11		13	2	11						2	11		16
22 × 17 dgr/bI	1	11	1				1	11	1				1	11	1	11	2	2	10	10	2	2	11					1	11	1	17
22 × 18 dgr/bII	11	1	1				1	1	11				11	1	1	2	2	20	2	2	2	20	2					1	1	11	18
22 × 19 ogr/b		11	2					2	11					11	2		2	11	13		2	11	13						2	11	19
22 × 20 lgr/w	5	1		5	1		1	5		1	5		11	2		6	1	5	13		2	11		6	1	5		2		11	20
22 × 21 dgr/wI	1	4	1	1	4	1	1	4	1	1	4	1	2	10	2	4	2	2	4	10	4	4	10	4	2	2	4	2	10	2	21
22 × 22 dgr/wII	3	2	1	3	2	1	1	2	3	1	2	3	8	4	2	2	2	8	2	4	4	10	4	2	2	8	2	2	11	8	22
22 × 23 ogr/w		5	1		5	1		1	5		1	5		11	2		1	5	6		2	11	13		1	5	6		2	11	23
22 × 24 ly/w				11	2					2	11		11	2						13	2	11		13	2	11		2	11		24
22 × 25 dy/wI				1	2	10				10	2	1	1	21	10					2	2	21	2	2	21	2	2	10	2	1	25
22 × 26 dy/wII				10	2	1				1	2	10	10	2	1					2	2	21	2	2	2	21	2	1	2	10	26
22 × 27 oy/w					11	2					2	11		11	2						2	11	13		11	2	13		2	11	27
22 × 28 sb/w							2	11		2	11					11	2			21	4			11	2	13		4	2		28
22 × 29 cb/w							1	6	5	1	6	5				5	1	5	1	11	2	11	2	5	1	5	1	2	13	11	29
22 × 30 ma/w								2	11		2	11						11	2			21	4			11	2		4	21	30
	1	2	3	4	5	6	7	8	9	10	11	12	13	14	15	16	17	18	19	20	21	22	23	24	25	26	27	28	29	30	

COLOUR PERCENTAGE TABLE No. 23 OLIVE GREEN / WHITE (OGR/W)

OGR/W = 23	1	2	3	4	5	6	7	8	9	10	11	12	13	14	15	16	17	18	19	20	21	22	23	24	25	26	27	28	29	30	
23 × 1 lgr		25												25				25				25									1
23 × 2 dgr		13	13											13	13			13	13			13	13								2
23 × 3 ogr			25												25				25				25								3
23 × 4 ly					25									25								25				25					4
23 × 5 dy					13	13								13	13							13	13			13	13				5
23 × 6 oy						25									25								25				25				6
23 × 7 sb								25									25				25								25		7
23 × 8 cb								13	13								13		13		13	13							13	13	8
23 × 9 ma									25										25			25								25	9
23 × 10 wsb											25										25				25				25		10
23 × 11 wcb											13	13									13		13		13		13		13	13	11
23 × 12 wma												25											25				25			25	12
23 × 13 lgr/y		13			13									25				13				25				13					13
23 × 14 dgr/y		6	6		6	6								13	13			6	6			13	13			6	6				14
23 × 15 ogr/y			13			13									25				13				25				13				15
23 × 16 lgr/b		13						13						13			13	13			13	13							13		16
23 × 17 dgr/bI		2	11					11	2					2	11		11	2	13		11	2	13						11	2	17
23 × 18 dgr/bII		11	2					2	11					11	2		2	11	13		2	11	13						2	11	18
23 × 19 ogr/b			13						13						13				25				25							13	19
23 × 20 lgr/w		6			6			6			6			13			6	6			13	13			6	6			13		20
23 × 21 dgr/wI		1	5		1	5		5	1		5	1		2	11		5	1	6		11	2	13		5	1	6		11	2	21
23 × 22 dgr/wII		5	1		5	1		1	5		1	5		11	2		1	5	6		2	11	13		1	5	6		2	11	22
23 × 23 ogr/w			6			6			6			6			13				13				25				13			13	23
23 × 24 ly/w					13						13			12							13	13			13	13			13		24
23 × 25 dy/wI					2	11					11	2		2	11						11	2	13		11	2	13		11	2	25
23 × 26 dy/wII					11	2					2	11		11	2						2	11	13		2	11	13		2	11	26
23 × 27 oy/w						13						13			13								25				25			13	27
23 × 28 sb/w								13			13						13				25				13				25		28
23 × 29 cb/w								6	6		6	6					6		6		13		13		6		6		13	13	29
23 × 30 ma/w									13			13							13				25				13			25	30
	1	2	3	4	5	6	7	8	9	10	11	12	13	14	15	16	17	18	19	20	21	22	23	24	25	26	27	28	29	30	

COLOUR PERCENTAGE TABLE No. 24 LIGHT YELLOW / WHITE (LY/W)

LY/W = 24	1	2	3	4	5	6	7	8	9	10	11	12	13	14	15	16	17	18	19	20	21	22	23	24	25	26	27	28	29	30	
24 × 1 lgr													50							50											1
24 × 2 dgr													25	25						25	25										2
24 × 3 ogr														50							50										3
24 × 4 ly				50																				50							4
24 × 5 dy				25	25																			25	25						5
24 × 6 oy					50																				50						6
24 × 7 sb																				50								50			7
24 × 8 cb																				25		25						25	25		8
24 × 9 ma																						50							50		9
24 × 10 wsb										50														50							10
24 × 11 wcb										25	25													25		25					11
24 × 12 wma											50															50					12
24 × 13 lgr/y				25									25							25				25							13
24 × 14 dgr/y				13	13								13	13						13	13			13	13						14
24 × 15 ogr/y					25									25							25				25						15
24 × 16 lgr/b													25							50								25			16
24 × 17 dgr/bI													4	21						25	21	4						21	4		17
24 × 18 dgr/bII													21	4						25	4	21						4	21		18
24 × 19 ogr/b														25							25	25							25		19
24 × 20 lgr/w				13						13			13							25				25				13			20
24 × 21 dgr/wI				2	11					11	2		2	11						13	21	4		13	21	4		11	2		21
24 × 22 dgr/wII				11	2					2	11		11	2						13	2	11		13	2	1		2	11		22
24 × 23 ogr/w					13						13			13							13	13			13	13			13		23
24 × 24 ly/w				25						25														50							24
24 × 25 dy/wI				4	21					21	4													25	21	4					25
24 × 26 dy/wII				21	4					4	21													25	4	21					26
24 × 27 oy/w					25						25														25	25					27
24 × 28 sb/w										25										25				25				25			28
24 × 29 cb/w										13	13									13		13		13		13		13	13		29
24 × 30 ma/w											25											25				25			25		30
	1	2	3	4	5	6	7	8	9	10	11	12	13	14	15	16	17	18	19	20	21	22	23	24	25	26	27	28	29	30	

COLOUR PERCENTAGE TABLE No. 25 DARK YELLOW / WHITE TYPE I (DY/WI)

DY/WI = 25	1	2	3	4	5	6	7	8	9	10	11	12	13	14	15	16	17	18	19	20	21	22	23	24	25	26	27	28	29	30	
25 × 1 lgr													8	42						42		8									1
25 × 2 dgr													4	25	21					21	21	4	4								2
25 × 3 ogr														8	42						42		8								3
25 × 4 ly				8	42																			42		8					4
25 × 5 dy				4	25	21																		21	21	4	4				5
25 × 6 oy					8	42																			42		8				6
25 × 7 sb																				8	42							42	8		7
25 × 8 cb																				4	21	4	21					21	25	4	8
25 × 9 ma																						8	42						42	8	9
25 × 10 wsb										42	8													8	42						10
25 × 11 wcb										21	25	4												4	21	4	21				11
25 × 12 wma											42	8														8	42				12
25 × 13 lgr/y				4	21								4	21						21		4		21		4					13
25 × 14 dgr/y				2	13	11							2	13	11					11	11	2	2	11	11	2	2				14
25,× 15 ogr/y					4	21								4	21						21		4		21		4				15
52 × 16 lgr/b													4	21						25	4	21						21	4		16
25 × 17 dgr/bI													2	13	11					13	21	4	13					11	13	2	17
25 × 18 dgr/bII													11	13	2					13	4	21	13					2	13	11	18
25 × 19 ogr/b														4	21						21	4	25						21	4	19
25 × 20 lgr/w				2	11					11	2		2	11						13	11	2		13	11	2		11	2		20
25 × 21 dgr/wI				1	10	2				2	10	1	1	10	2					2	20	2	2	2	20	2	2	2	10	1	21
25 × 22 dgr/wII				1	2	10				10	2	1	1	2	10					2	2	20	2	2	2	20	2	10	2	1	22
25 × 23 ogr/w					2	11					11	2		2	11						11	2	13		11	2	13		11	2	23
55 × 24 ly/w				4	21					21	4													25	21	4					24
25 × 25 dy/wI				2	5	18				18	5	2												5	36	5	5				25
25 × 26 dy/wII				2	21	2				2	21	2												21	4	4	21				26
25 × 27 oy/w					4	21					21	4													21	4	25				27
25 × 28 sb/w										21	4									4	21			4	21			21	4		28
25 × 29 cb/w										11	13	2								2	11	2	11	2	11	2	11	11	13	2	29
22 × 30 ma/w											21	4										4	21			4	21		21	4	30
	1	2	3	4	5	6	7	8	9	10	11	12	13	14	15	16	17	18	19	20	21	22	23	24	25	26	27	28	29	30	

COLOUR PERCENTAGE TABLE No. 26 DARK YELLOW / WHITE TYPE II (DY/WII)

DY/WII = 26	1	2	3	4	5	6	7	8	9	10	11	12	13	14	15	16	17	18	19	20	21	22	23	24	25	26	27	28	29	30	
26 × 1 lgr													42	8						8		42									1
26 × 2 dgr													21	25	4					4	4	21	21								2
26 × 3 ogr														42	8						8		42								3
26 × 4 ly				42	8																			8		42					4
26 × 5 dy				21	25	4																		4	4	21	21				5
26 × 6 oy					42	8																			42		8				6
26 × 7 sb																				42	8							8	42		7
26 × 8 cb																				21	4	21	4					4	25	21	8
26 × 9 ma																						42	8						8	42	9
26 × 10 wsb										8	42													42	8						10
26 × 11 wcb										4	25	21												21	4	21	4				11
26 × 12 wma											8	42														42	8				12
26 × 13 lgr/y				21	4								21	4						4		21		4		21					13
26 × 14 dgr/y				11	13	2							11	13	2					2	2	11	11	2	2	11	11				14
26 × 15 ogr/y					21	4								21	4						4		21		4		21				15
26 × 16 lgr/b													21	4						25	4	21						4	21		16
26 × 17 dgr/bI													11	13	2					13	4	21	13					2	13	11	17
26 × 18 dgr/bII													11	13	2					13	4	21	13					2	13	11	18
26 × 19 ogr/b														21	4						4	21	25						4	21	19
26 × 20 lgr/w				11	2					2	11		11	2						13	2	11		13	2	11		2	11		20
26 × 21 dgr/wI				2	10	1				1	10	2	2	10	1					10	2	2	10	10	2	2	10	1	10	2	21
26 × 22 dgr/wII				10	2	1				1	2	10	10	2	1					2	2	20	2	2	2	20	2	1	2	10	22
26 × 23 ogr/w					11	2					2	11		11	2						2	11	13		2	11	13		2	11	23
26 × 24 ly/w				21	4					4	21													25	4	21					24
26 × 25 dy/wI				2	21	2				2	21	2												21	4	4	21				25
26 × 26 dy/wII				13	5	2				2	5	18												5	5	36	5				26
26 × 27 oy/w					21	4					4	21													4	21	25				27
26 × 28 sb/w										4	21									21	4			21	4			4	21		28
26 × 29 cb/w										2	13	11								11	2	11	2	11	2	11	2	2	13	11	29
26 × 30 ma/w											4	21										21	4			21	4		4	21	30
	1	2	3	4	5	6	7	8	9	10	11	12	13	14	15	16	17	18	19	20	21	22	23	24	25	26	27	28	29	30	

COLOUR PERCENTAGE TABLE No. 27 OLIVE YELLOW / WHITE (OY/W)

OY/W = 27	1	2	3	4	5	6	7	8	9	10	11	12	13	14	15	16	17	18	19	20	21	22	23	24	25	26	27	28	29	30	
27 × 1 lgr														50								50									1
27 × 2 dgr														25	25							25	25								2
27 × 3 ogr															50								50								3
27 × 4 ly					50																				50						4
27 × 5 dy					25	25																			25	25					5
27 × 6 oy						50																				50					6
27 × 7 sb																					50							50			7
27 × 8 cb																					25		25					25		25	8
27 × 9 ma																							50							50	9
27 × 10 wsb											50														50						10
27 × 11 wcb											25	25													25		25				11
27 × 12 wma												50															50				12
27 × 13 lgr/y					25									25								25				25					13
27 × 14 dgr/y					13	13								13	13							13	13			13	13				14
27 × 15 ogr/y						25									25								25				25				15
27 × 16 lgr/b														25							25	25							25		16
27 × 17 dgr/bI														4	21						21	4	25						21	4	17
27 × 18 dgr/bII														21	4						4	21	25						4	21	18
27 × 19 ogr/b															25								50							25	19
27 × 20 lgr/w					13						13			13							13	13			13	13			13		20
27 × 21 dgr/wI					2	11					11	2		2	11						11	2	13		11	2	13		11	2	21
27 × 22 dgr/wII					11	2					2	11		11	2						2	11	13		2	11	13		2	11	22
27 × 23 ogr/w						13						13			13								25				25			13	23
27 × 24 ly/w					25						25														25	25					24
27 × 25 dy/wI					4	21					21	4													21	4	25				25
27 × 26 dy/wII					21	4					4	21													4	21	25				26
27 × 27 oy/w						25						25															50				27
27 × 28 sb/w											25										25				25				25		28
27 × 29 cb/w											13	13									13		13		13		13		13	13	29
27 × 30 ma/w												25											25				25			25	30
	1	2	3	4	5	6	7	8	9	10	11	12	13	14	15	16	17	18	19	20	21	22	23	24	25	26	27	28	29	30	

COLOUR PERCENTAGE TABLE No. 28 SKY BLUE / WHITE (SB/W)

SB/W = 28	1	2	3	4	5	6	7	8	9	10	11	12	13	14	15	16	17	18	19	20	21	22	23	24	25	26	27	28	29	30	
28 × 1 lgr																50				50											1
28 × 2 dgr																25	25			25	25										2
28 × 3 ogr																	50				50										3
28 × 4 ly																				50				50							4
28 × 5 dy																				25	25			25	25						5
28 × 6 oy																					50				50						6
28 × 7 sb							50																					50			7
28 × 8 cb							25	25																				25	25		8
28 × 9 ma								50																					50		9
28 × 10 wsb										50																		50			10
28 × 11 wcb										25	25																	25	25		11
28 × 12 wma											50																		50		12
28 × 13 lgr/y																25				50				25							13
28 × 14 dgr/y																13	13			25	25			13	13						14
28 × 15 ogr/y																	25				50				25						15
28 × 16 lgr/b							25									25				25								25			16
28 × 17 dgr/bI							21	4								4	21			4	21							21	4		17
28 × 18 dgr/bII							4	21								21	4			21	4							4	21		18
28 × 19 ogr/b								25									25				25								25		19
28 × 20 lgr/w							13			13						13				25				13				25			20
28 × 21 dgr/wI							11	2		11	2					2	11			4	21			2	11			21	4		21
28 × 22 dgr/wII							2	11		2	11					11	2			21	4			11	2			4	21		22
28 × 23 ogr/w								13			13						13				25				13				25		23
28 × 24 ly/w										25										25				25				25			24
28 × 25 dy/wI										21	4									4	21			4	21			21	4		25
28 × 26 dy/wII										4	21									21	4			21	4			4	21		26
28 × 27 oy/w											25										25				25				25		27
28 × 28 sb/w							25			25																		50			28
28 × 29 cb/w							13	13		13	13																	25	25		29
28 × 30 ma/w								25			25																		50		30
	1	2	3	4	5	6	7	8	9	10	11	12	13	14	15	16	17	18	19	20	21	22	23	24	25	26	27	28	29	30	

COLOUR PERCENTAGE TABLE No. 29 COBALT / WHITE (CB/W)

CB/W = 29	1	2	3	4	5	6	7	8	9	10	11	12	13	14	15	16	17	18	19	20	21	22	23	24	25	26	27	28	29	30	
29 × 1 lgr																25		25		25		25									1
29 × 2 dgr																13	13	13	13	13	13	13	13								2
29 × 3 ogr																	25		25		25		25								3
29 × 4 ly																				25		25		25		25					4
29 × 5 dy																				13	13	13	13	13	13	13	13				5
29 × 6 oy																					25		25		25		25				6
29 × 7 sb							25	25																				25	25		7
29 × 8 cb							13	25	13																			13	25	13	8
29 × 9 ma								25	25																				25	25	9
29 × 10 wsb										25	25																	25	25		10
29 × 11 wcb										13	25	13																13	25	13	11
29 × 12 wma											25	25																	25	25	12
29 × 13 lgr/y																13		13		25		25		13		13					13
29 × 14 dgr/y																6	6	6	6	13	13	13	13	6	6	6	6				14
29 × 15 ogr/y																	13		13		25		25		13		13				15
29 × 16 lgr/b							13	13								13		13		13		13						13	13		16
29 × 17 dgr/bI							11	13	2							2	11	2	11	2	11	2	11					11	13	2	17
29 × 18 dgr/bII							2	13	11							11	2	11	2	11	2	11	2					2	13	11	18
29 × 19 ogr/b								13	13								13		13		13		13						13	13	19
29 × 20 lgr/w							6	6		6	6					6		6		13		13		6		6		13	13		20
29 × 21 dgr/wI							5	6	1	5	6	1				1	5	1	5	2	11	2	11	1	5	1	5	11	13	2	21
29 × 22 dgr/wII							1	6	5	1	6	5				5	1	5	1	11	2	11	2	5	1	5	1	2	13	11	22
29 × 23 ogr/w								6	6		6	6					6		6		13		13		6		6		13	13	23
29 × 24 ly/w										13	13									13		13		13		13		13	13		24
29 × 25 dy/wI										11	13	2								2	11	2	11	2	11	2	11	11	13	2	25
29 × 26 dy/wII										2	13	11								11	2	11	2	11	2	11	2	2	13	11	26
29 × 27 oy/w											13	13									13		13		13		13		13	13	27
29 × 28 sb/w							13	13		13	13																	25	25		28
29 × 29 cb/w							6	13	6	6	13	6																13	25	13	29
29 × 30 ma/w								13	13		13	13																	25	25	30
	1	2	3	4	5	6	7	8	9	10	11	12	13	14	15	16	17	18	19	20	21	22	23	24	25	26	27	28	29	30	

COLOUR PERCENTAGE TABLE No. 30 MAUVE / WHITE (MA/W)

MA/W = 30	1	2	3	4	5	6	7	8	9	10	11	12	13	14	15	16	17	18	19	20	21	22	23	24	25	26	27	28	29	30	
30 × 1 lgr																		50				50									1
30 × 2 dgr																		25	25			25	25								2
30 × 3 ogr																			50				50								3
30 × 4 ly																						50				50					4
30 × 5 dy																						25	25			25	25				5
30 × 6 oy																							50				50				6
30 × 7 sb								50																					50		7
30 × 8 cb								25	25																				25	25	8
30 × 9 ma									50																					50	9
30 × 10 wsb											50																		50		10
30 × 11 wcb											25	25																	25	25	11
30 × 12 wma												50																		50	12
30 × 13 lgr/y																		25				50				25					13
30 × 14 dgr/y																		13	13			25	25			13	13				14
30 × 15 ogr/y																			25				50				25				15
30 × 16 lgr/b								25										25				25							25		16
30 × 17 dgr/bI								21	4									4	21			4	21						21	4	17
30 × 18 dgr/bII								4	21									21	4			21	4						4	21	18
30 × 19 ogr/b									25										25				25							25	19
30 × 20 lgr/w								13			13							13				25				13			25		20
30 × 21 dgr/wI								11	2		11	2						2	11			4	21			2	11		21	4	21
30 × 22 dgr/wII								2	11		2	11						11	2			21	4			11	2		4	21	22
30 × 23 ogr/w									13			13							13				25				13			25	23
30 × 24 ly/w											25											25				25			25		24
30 × 25 dy/wI											21	4										4	21			4	21		21	4	25
30 × 26 dy/wII											4	21										21	4			21	4		4	21	26
30 × 27 oy/w												25											25				25			25	27
30 × 28 sb/w								25			25																		50		28
30 × 29 cb/w								13	13		13	13																	25	25	29
30 × 30 ma/w									25			25																		50	30
	1	**2**	**3**	**4**	**5**	**6**	**7**	**8**	**9**	**10**	**11**	**12**	**13**	**14**	**15**	**16**	**17**	**18**	**19**	**20**	**21**	**22**	**23**	**24**	**25**	**26**	**27**	**28**	**29**	**30**	

BIBLIOGRAPHY

American Cage Birds Magazine: Audubon Publ. Co, Chicago, USA.
Dr. M. D. S. Armour: *Exhibition Budgerigars:* Iliffe Press, London.
Dr. M. D. S. Armour: *Inbreeding Budgerigars.* Iliffe Press, London.
Avicultural Magazine: Avicultural Society, London.
The Duke of Bedford: *Homing Budgerigars.* Iliffe Press, London.
E. W. Brooks: *Development of color in Budgerigars.*
Budgerigar Bulletins: Budgerigar Society.
Budgerigar Mating and Colour Expectations: Budgerigar Society.
R. Carpentier: *La perruche ondulée*, Boubée & Cie, Paris.
F. A. E. Crew: *Genetics of the Budgerigar.*
Dr. Hans Duncker: *Verebungslehre für Kleinvogelzüchter*, Leipzig.
Curt af Enehjelm: *Das Buch vom Wellensittich*, Pfungstadt.
Mme. Feuillée-Billot: *Perroquets, Perruches, Colombes*, La Maison Rustique, Paris.
M. L. and Flora Flowers: *Parrakeets, their Care and Breeding*, Reseda, USA.
M. L. and Flora Flowers: *Teaching the Budgerigar to Talk*, Reseda, USA.
N. Grasl: *Der sprechende Wellensittich*, Philler Verlag, Minden.
N. Grasl: *Der Wellensittich, seine Pflege und Zucht*, Philler Verlag, Minden.
N. Grasl: *Verebungsregeln für den Wellensittichzüchter.*
K. Kokemüller: *Farbentabelle für Wellensittiche.*
M. Legendre: *La perruche ondulée et les inséparables*, Boubée & Cie, Paris.
Marie Murray: *The Talking Budgie*, Audubon Publ. Co, Chicago, USA.
Karl Neunzig: *Der Wellensittich*, Magdeburg.
B. Ragotzi: *Freude am Wellensittich*, Reimer Verlag, Berlin.
C. H. Rogers, *A-Z Budgerigars* Max Parrish, London.
C. H. Rogers, *Budgerigars*, Foyles, London.
C. H. Rogers, *The World of Budgerigars*, Nimrod Book Services.
A. Rutgers: *Tropische Volièrevogels*, Uitg. L. S. M., Joppe.
J. Schräpel: *Die beste Art*, Wellensittiche zu zücheten.
Dr. Hans Steiner: *Vererbungsstudien am Wellensittich, Orell Füssli*, Zürich.

Marquess of Tavistock: *Parrots and parrot-like birds*, F. V. White & Co, London.

Taylor and Warner, *Genetics for Budgerigar Breeders*, Iliffe Press, London.

H. Völker: *Melopsittacus Vererbungskreis*, Bad Kreuznach.

W. Watmough: *The Cult of the Budgerigar*, Nimrod Book Services.

A. Wilson: *Talking Budgerigars*, Iliffe Press.

INDEX

Abrahams, 10
Albinos, 20, 125, 126, 160, 175, 184, 190, 193, 200, **Pl. 26**
Antwerp Zoo, 9
Australia, 7, 8, 9, 10, 98, 99, 114,
Australian Dominant Pieds *see* Dominant Australian Pieds
Australian White-flighted Opaline Sky Blue, **Pl. 37**
Australian Yellow-flighted Light Green, **Pl. 58**
Aviaries, 103–10, 112, 113, 130

Banded Pied, 190, 191, 192, **Pls. 53–6**
Betcherrygar, 5
Birds of Australia, The, 5, 9
Blue, 11, 15, 157, 170, 179, 184
Breeding cages, 134, 137
Breeding register, 125, 126, 127
Brehm, 6, 149
Budgerigar Society, 139, 142

Cage (*and Aviary*) Birds, 136, 139, 171
Cages, 100–3, 110, 137
Caked feet, 123
Canary seed, 115, 116, 117
Cayley, 7, 8
Ceres, 150
Chromosome, 126, 157
Cinnamon, 160, 175, 200, 203
Cinnamon Cobalt, 18
Cinnamon Dark Green, 18, **Pl. 19**
Cinnamon Grey, 19, **Pl. 41**
Cinnamon Grey Green, 18, **Pl. 18**
Cinnamon Greywing Cobalt, **Pl. 42**
Cinnamon Greywing Dark Green, **Pl. 20**
Cinnamon Light Green, 17–18
Cinnamon Light Grey, **Pl. 68**
Cinnamon Mauve, 18
Cinnamon Olive Green, 18
Cinnamon Sky Blue, 18
Cinnamon Violet Cobalt, 18
Circular Crested Light Green, **Pl. 66**
Clearbody, 175, 201, 203
Clearflight Cobalt, 29
Clearflight Dark Green, 28
Clearflight Grey, 30
Clearflight Grey Green, 28
Clearflight Light Green, 28, Pl. 57, **Pl. 58**
Clearflight Mauve, 29
Clearflight Olive Green, 28
Clearflight Skyblue, 28
Clearflight Violet Cobalt, 30
Clearflighted, 162, 184, 186
Clearwing Budgerigar Breeders Association, 167
Clearwings, 164, 167–70, 172
Cobalt, 11, 15, 125, 160, 177, 202, 205, **Pl. 8**
Cold, 120
Colour Percentage Tables, 205–37
Colour Plates, 32
Colour Standards, 12–32
Cremer, Gen. Con.C.H., 156
Crestbred, 195, 196
Crested, 31–2, 194–7, **Pls. 66–68**
Crested B.C. Handbook, 197
Crests, 31
Crewe, Prof. F.A.E., 156
Cuttle-fish bone, 117, 134

Danish Recessive Pieds *see* Recessive Danish Pieds

Dark, 11, 158, 159, 161, 163, 164, 177
Dark-eyed Clear inheritance, 188
Dark-eyed Clear Whites, 30, 187–9
Dark-eyed Clear Yellows, 29, 187–9, **Pl. 59**
Dark-eyed Clears, 162, 172, 184, 187–9
Dark Green, 8, 14, 158, 160, **Pl. 2**
Dark Green/Blue Type II, 160
DD, Dd, dd, 159
Degeneration, 122
Dettol, 123
Diseases, 118–23
Dominant, 157–9, 161–4, 167, 177, 178, 184, 185, 186, 190, 194, 196
Dominant Australian Pieds, 161, 162, 190–3, **Pl. 53–6:** inheritance, 191
Dominant Clear-flighted, 162
Dominant Pied Cobalt, 27
Dominant Pied Dark Green, 27
Dominant Pied Grey, 28
Dominant Pied Greywing Cobalt, **Pl. 51**
Dominant Pied Light Green, 26–7, **Pl. 49**
Dominant Pied Mauve, 27
Dominant Pied Olive Green, 27
Dominant Pied Opaline Dark Green, **Pl. 52**
Dominant Pied Skyblue, 27, **Pl. 50**
Dominant Pied Violet Cobalt, 28
Double factor, 172
Duncker, Dr. H., 156
Dutch Pieds, 184–6

Egg binding, 122
Enehjelm, Herr C. af, 181
Engelhardt, 6
English Fallows, 174, 175
English Grey, 203
Establissements Bastide, 9
Establissements Ornithologiques Blanchard, 9
Eucalyptus, 6, 7

Fallow Cobalt, 19, **Pl. 24**
Fallow Dark Green, 19
Fallow Grey, 20
Fallow Grey Green, 19
Fallow Light Green, 19, **Pl. 23**
Fallow Mauve, 20, 159
Fallow Olive Green, 19, 176
Fallow Opaline Grey, 176
Fallow Sky Blue, 19, **Pl. 40**
Fallow Violet Cobalt, 20
Fallows, 167, 174–6, 203: inheritance, 174, 175
Faults, 143, 144, 145
Feather plucking, 131
Foster parents, 131
Full-bodied coloured Greywings, 167, 202
Full-circular crest, 31, 194, 196, **Pl. 66**

Genes, 157
Genetics for Budgerigar Breeders, 156
Genotype, 157
German Fallows, 174, 175
Golden-faced, 159, 173
Gould, John, 5, 8, 9
Grasparkiet, 5
Grass Parakeets, 6
Green, 8, 10, 11, 14, 159, 163, 166, 169, 179, 184, **Pls. 1–4**
Green food, 116, 134
Grey, 15, 161, 166, 172, 183, 199
Grey Green, 14, 166, **Pl. 4**
Greywing Cobalt, 17, **Pl. 39**
Greywing Dark Green, 16
Greywing Grey, 17
Greywing Grey Green, 17
Greywing Light Green, 16, 159, 164, 165, 166, **Pl. 15**
Greywing Light Green/Yellow, 165
Greywing Olive Green, 17
Greywing Skyblue, 17, 165, 166, **Pl. 16**
Greywing Violet Cobalt, 17
Greywing Yellows, 199
Greywings, 164, 201, 202, 203

Grit, 103, 116

Half-circular crests, 31, 194, 196, **Pl. 67**
Hospital cage, 121

Ideal Budgerigar, 13, 132, 142, 143
Intestinal trouble, 120

Jamrach, 9
Judge(s), 139, 143

Lacewing Light Green, 30
Lacewing Olive Green, 30
Lacewing White, 30, **Pl. 62**
Lacewing Yellow, 30, **Pl. 63**
Lacewings, 160, 190, 200
La Peruche Ondulée, 148
Lethal factor, 195
Lice, 131
Light Green, 10, 12, 158, 159, 163, 164, 168, 199, 200, 206, Pl. 1, **Pl. 66**
Light Green/Blue, 157, 158, 159
Light Green/Yellow, 164, 165
Light Green/Yellow-wing, 168
Light Grey, **Pl. 11**
Light Yellow, 8, 10, 14, 163, 164, 165, 166, 206, **Pl. 5**, **Pl. 14**
Linnean Society, 9
Long-flighted, 143
Lutino, 10–11, 20, 126, 127, 160, 175, 184, 190, 192, 193, 200, **Pl. 25**

Mallee shrub, 6
Mantle, 170
Mauve, 11, 15, 127, 180, 188, **Pl. 9**
Melopsittacus Undulatus, 5, 8
Mendel, Gregor, 156
Mendelian, 158, 187
Millet, 115, 116, 117, 151
Millet, spray, 115
Moult, 103, 104, 122
Mutant I, 171
Mutant II, 171

Nesting boxes, 98–101, 104, 110, 112, 124, 127, 130, 131, 133, 134, 138,
Normal(s), 163–5, 181, 182, 185, 191, 192, 195, 196, 202

Olive Green, 14, 158, 163, 180, 188, 200, 206, **Pl. 3**
Olive Yellow, 14, **Pl. 6**
Opaline, 125, 160, 169, 193, 200, 203
Opaline Cinnamon Cobalt, 23, **Pl. 33**
Opaline Cinnamon Dark Green, 22, **Pl. 31**
Opaline Cinnamon Grey, 23, **Pl. 34**
Opaline Cinnamon Grey Green, 22, **Pl. 32**
Opaline Cinnamon Light Green, 21–2
Opaline Cinnamon Mauve, 23
Opaline Cinnamon Olive Green, 22
Opaline Cinnamon Skyblue, 22
Opaline Cinnamon Violet Cobalt, 23
Opaline Clearwings, 169
Opaline Cobalt, 21
Opaline Dark Green, 20
Opaline Grey, 21
Opaline Grey Green, 21, **Pl. 28**
Opaline Greywing Cobalt, 24
Opaline Greywing Dark Green, 23
Opaline Greywing Grey, 24
Opaline Greywing Light Green, 23
Opaline Greywing Mauve, 24
Opaline Greywing Olive Green, 24
Opaline Greywing Skyblue, 24
Opaline Greywing Violet Cobalt, 24
Opaline Lacewing White, **Pl. 62**
Opaline Light Green, 20, **Pl. 27**
Opaline Mauve, 21, 125, **Pl. 43**
Opaline Olive Green, 21
Opaline Sky Blue, 21, 125, **Pl. 29**
Opaline Violet Cobalt, 21, **Pl. 30**
Opaline Whitewing Cobalt, **Pl. 64**
Opaline Whitewing Sky Blue, **Pl. 65**

Opaline Yellow, 14
Opaline Yellow-wing Dark Green, **Pl. 35**
Open-air flight, 100

Perruche ondule, 5
Phenotype, 157
Pied Budgerigar Society of G.B., 182, 190
Pied (Clear-flighted) Grey, 28
Pied (Clear-flighted) Light Green *see* Clearflight Light Green
Pied (Dominant) *see* Dominant Pieds
Pied (Recessive) *see* Recessive Pieds
Plum-coloured eyes, 25–6, 181, 187, 192
Psittacosis, 118, 119

Rainbows, 170, 172, 173, 201, 202, **Pl. 64**, **Pl. 65**
Recessive, 159, 163, 167, 185
Recessive Brown-wing, 203
Recessive Danish Pied, 26, 161–2, 181–3, 187–90, 192, 193: inheritance, 181, 182
Recessive Pied Cinnamon Violet Cobalt, **Pl. 46**
Recessive Pied Cobalt, 26, **Pl. 45**
Recessive Pied Dark Green, 25
Recessive Pied Grey, 26
Recessive Pied Grey Green, 25
Recessive Pied Light Green, 25, **Pl. 44**
Recessive Pied Mauve, 26
Recessive Pied Olive Green, 25
Recessive Pied Opaline Dark Green, **Pl. 47**
Recessive Pied Skyblue, 25–6
Recessive Pied Violet Cobalt, 26
Recessive Pied Yellow-faced Sky Blue, **Pl. 48**
Red, 12, 203
Red-eyed Lacewings, 200
Redmite, 131
Rings, 128

Saddle-back, 198
Scale of Points, 140, 141, 142
Scaly face, 123
Seed, 114, 115, 117
Seed hoppers, 134, 135
Self, 170
Sex-linked, 159, 160
Shaw, 5
Show Cage, Standard, 145, 146
Single factor, 171, 172, 177, 179, 191
Skyblue, 15, 160, 161, 165, 169, 177, 179, **Pl. 7**, **Pl. 38**, **Pl. 67**
Slate, 160, 172, 199
Slate Skyblue, **Pl. 60**
Spangle Cobalt, 32
Spangle Dark Green, 31
Spangle Grey, 32
Spangle Grey Green, 31
Spangle Light Green, 31
Spangle Mauve, 32
Spangle Olive, 31
Spangle Skyblue, 31–2
Spangles, 198
Split, 125, 126, 157, 168, 181, 182, 184, 190, 206

Toulouse, 9
Tufted, 194, 196
Tufted Crest Cinnamon Light Grey, **Pl. 68**

Uccle, 10, 11
Undulated Grass Parakeet, 5

Vertigo, 123
Violet character, 161, 177–80
Violet Cinnamons, 180
Violet Clearwings, 180
Violet Cobalt, 15, 166, 178, **Pl. 10**
Violet Dark Green, **Pl. 61**
Violet Green, 161, 179, 180
Violet Grey, 179
Violet inheritance, 178
Violet Mauve, 179
Violet Opalines, 180

Violet Sky Blue, 179
Visual Violet, 177, 178, 179: *see also* Violet Cobalt

Washing, 146
White, 11, 15, 167
White-flighted Grey, 28
White-flighted Opaline Cobalt, **Pl. 36**
White-flighted Sky Blue, **Pl. 37**
White Sky Blue, 169, **Pl. 12**
Whitewing, 15, 118, 169, **Pl. 12**
Whitewing Sky Blue, 168, **Pl. 17**
Wightwing Sky Blue/White, 169
Whitewing Violet Cobalt, **Pl. 22**

Yellow, 10–11, 14, **Pls. 5–6**
Yellow-faced, 24–5, 159, 169, 171–3, 183, 184, 188, **Pls. 38–43**
Yellow-faced Blue, 171–3, 201, 202
Yellow-faced Cinnamon Fallow White, 175
Yellow-faced Cinnamon Grey, **Pl. 41**
Yellow-faced Cinnamon Greywing Cobalt, **Pl. 42**
Yellow-faced Clearwings, 169
Yellow-faced Fallow Sky Blue, **Pl. 40**
Yellow-faced Greywing Cobalt, **Pl. 39**
Yellow-faced Opaline Mauve, **Pl. 43**
Yellow-faced Opaline Whitewings, 201, 202, **Pls. 64–65**
Yellow-faced Sky Blue, **Pl. 38**, **Pl. 48**
Yellow-faced White Blue, 201
Yellow-faced Whitewings, 169
Yellow-flighted *see* Clearflights
Yellow-wing Dark Green, 16, **Pl. 21**
Yellow-wing Grey Green, 16
Yellow-wing Light Green, 16, 165, 167, 168, **Pl. 13**
Yellow-wing Light Green/Yellow, 165, 168
Yellow-wing Olive Green, 16
Yellow-wings, 167–70